Care for All

Effective Patient Communication for Healthcare Workers

Hiroaki Tanaka / Kaoru Masago

写真提供：Istock Photo
画像提供：DMM 英会話
　　　　　（Units 1-15 Pronunciation Box画像）

音声ファイルのダウンロード/ストリーミング

CD マーク表示がある箇所は，音声を弊社 HP より無料でダウンロード/ストリーミングすることができます。下記 URL の書籍詳細ページに音声ダウンロードアイコンがございますのでそちらから自習用音声としてご活用ください。

https://seibido.co.jp/ad724

Care for All
―Effective Patient Communication for Healthcare Workers―

Copyright © 2025 by Hiroaki Tanaka, Kaoru Masago

All rights reserved for Japan.
No part of this book may be reproduced in any form
without permission from Seibido Co., Ltd.

はしがき

　本書は看護やリハビリテーションを学ぶ学生のみなさんのための，病院での英会話表現を学ぶテキストです。本書での会話はサブタイトル Patient Communication とあるように，外国人患者さんと未来の医療従事者であるみなさんが上手にそして効果的に意思疎通ができるようになることを目指しています。

　本書の特徴は，専門用語の使用はあえて抑え，高校までで学習した簡単で分かりやすい英語表現を使うことで，中学・高校と英語が苦手だった人でも学びやすいように工夫しました点です。英語での専門用語の習得は将来的な目標として重要ですが，まずは第一歩として，自分の知っている英語表現を使って外国人患者さんと積極的にコミュニケーションをとってみましょう。

　また本書は英語が苦手な人でも学びやすいように，積み上げ式に理解を深める構成になっています。まず「A. Warm Up」で各テーマの導入を行った後，語彙を学習し，そのUnitでポイントになる発音の練習を行います。それを踏まえて，「C. Useful Expressions for Patient Communication」で英会話の表現を学びながら，簡単な文法事項の確認を行います。続く「D. Patient Communication」で臨床現場を意識した短めの英会話の演習があります。その後，英文読解を通して各テーマへの理解を深めた後，「F. Role Play」で患者と医療従事者に分かれたコミュニケーション演習を行います。このように本書は基礎的な内容理解を基に，それを英語でのコミュニケーションにまで発展できるように工夫しています。

　本書のもう一つの特徴は，テーマごとの英語表現を学習するだけでなく，それに関連する医療に関する豆知識や実際の臨床現場で働く先輩からのメッセージを取り入れた点です。例えば「D. Patient Communication」の「notes」では，英単語の意味の注釈だけでなく，それにまつわる日本と海外での医療の違い，異文化理解，そして発展的な医療の知識も学習できるようになっています。また各 Unit の最後には「臨床現場からのメッセージ」として，実際に病院などの臨床現場で働くみなさんの先輩にあたる看護師や技師からのアドバイスも掲載しています。医療は座学で学んだ理論や技術を臨床に応用する学問分野です。テキストで学んだ内容が実際の医療現場ではどのように活かされているのか先輩のメッセージから読み取ってください。

　本書は看護師や技師の先生方に監修していただき，できるだけリアルな患者と医療従事者とのコミュニケーションになるようにしました。もちろん入門用のテキストですから，表現は分かりやすくシンプルにしています。未来の看護師や技師としての自分をイメージしながら学習を進めると，学習もリアルなものになるでしょう。

Care for All
Effective Patient Communication for Healthcare Workers

目次

UNIT 1 p.2
Is this your first visit to this hospital?
挨拶と窓口対応をしてみよう。

UNIT 2 p.7
What's the matter with you?
身体のどこに問題があるのか尋ねてみよう。

UNIT 3 p.12
I'm going to take a blood sample
採血をしよう。

UNIT 4 p.17
Let me explain our daily routine
入院生活の流れを説明しよう。

UNIT 5 p.22
I'm going to ask you about your lifestyle habits
生活習慣や宗教上の制限を確認しよう。

UNIT 6 p.27
Have you had any surgeries before?
病歴を確認しよう。

UNIT 7 p.32
Do you have any allergies?
アレルギーの有無を確認しよう。

UNIT 8　　p.37

How would you describe the pain?
どのような痛みがあるか確認しよう。

UNIT 9　　p.42

How much can you move your legs?
可動域を確認しよう。

UNIT 10　　p.47

Let's start practicing getting into the wheelchair
車いすへの移乗介助をしよう。

UNIT 11　　p.52

Let's make the walks longer
歩行トレーニングをしよう。

UNIT 12　　p.57

You're from Australia, aren't you?
患者さんと雑談をしよう。

UNIT 13　　p.62

Are you Ms. Brown?
家族の方とコミュニケーションをとろう。

UNIT 14　　p.67

Rehabilitation can be challenging
リハビリがうまくいかず落ち込む患者さんを励まそう。

UNIT 15　　p.72

By working together, we can ease your concerns
手術前で不安な患者さんを元気づけよう。

巻末付録：指差し英会話　　p.77

本書の使い方

A Warm Up

各 Unit のメインテーマについて日本語で示し問題提起をしています。学習を始める前に良く読んで考えてみましょう。また，ペアやグループで話し合ってみるのも良いでしょう。

B Vocabulary

各 Unit それぞれのキーワードとも言える語句の確認です。意味を確認しておきましょう。また音声で発音の確認もしましょう。

Pronunciation Box ///

Vocabulary に登場する語句に関連する発音のポイントを紹介しています。ポイントに注意しながら各自で練習をしてみましょう。

C Useful Expressions for Patient Communication

Healthcare Worker と患者の間でよく使われる表現を各 Unit ごとに確認しましょう。まずは日本語ではどんな意味になるのか確認し，発音に注意しながら声に出して読んでみましょう。

Grammar Box

Useful Expressions for Patient Communication で取り上げた英文の文法について確認しましょう。練習問題も用意していますので理解できたかどうかの確認をしましょう。

D Patient Communication

各 Unit のメインの会話となっています。ここまでの学習を踏まえてまずは会話文を完成し，その後音声を繰り返し聞いて Healthcare Worker の表現も患者の表現も使えるようにしましょう。

E Reading Comprehension

ここでは英文読解に挑戦しましょう。各 Unit のここまでの学習をヒントに英文を読み，設問に答えて理解力を確かめましょう。

F Role Play

メインの会話とは違った場面設定で身に付けた表現がうまく使えるか確かめましょう。

p.77 からの指さし英会話

Role Play を更に発展させた演習活動ができます。また臨床に出てからも役に立つ表現が満載です。学習が終わってからも本書を臨床現場に持っていけば，外国人患者とのコミュニケーションに役立ちます。

vi

《 Units 1-15 》

UNIT 1

Is this your first visit to this hospital?

A Warm Up

患者さんは病院に到着したら，まず受付で各種手続きをします。その際にどのようなものが必要でしょうか？また，日本国籍を持たない外国人の場合はどうでしょうか？ペアで考えましょう。

B Vocabulary

CD 02

以下の英単語の意味を選択肢の日本語を記号で選びましょう。

1. consider [　]　　2. prepare [　]
3. fill out [　]　　4. patient form [　]
5. overseas travel insurance [　]　　6. medical insurance card [　]

選択肢
a. 問診票　b. 医療保険証　c. 海外旅行保険　d. 考慮する　e. 記入する　f. 準備する

Pronunciation Box

[f] と [v]

patient form や overseas travel insurance にそれぞれ [f] と [v] の発音が含まれています。違いに注意して丁寧に発音しましょう。
[f]：無声音なので，上の前歯を下の唇に当てながら息を吐き出して発音します。
[v]：有声音なので，[f] の発音のまま喉を震わせて音を出します。

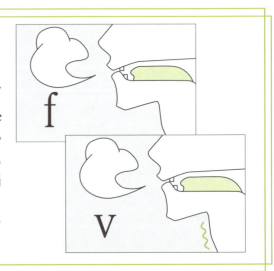

• Unit 1 • Is this your first visit to this hospital?

C Useful Expressions for Patient Communication

以下は患者さんとの英語コミュニケーションでよく使用される表現です。正しい意味を選択肢から選びましょう。

Healthcare Worker の表現

1. Is this your first visit to this hospital? [　]
2. Do you have a Japanese medical insurance card? [　]
3. Please fill out this patient form. [　]

Patient の表現

4. I'd like to see a doctor. [　]
5. I have overseas travel insurance. [　]
6. Here is my card. [　]

選択肢

a. 日本の医療保険証をお持ちですか？
b. こちらの問診票にご記入ください。
c. この病院に来るのは初めてですか？
d. これが私のカードです。
e. 医師に診てもらいたいです。
f. 海外旅行保険に加入しています。

Grammar Box　　　　　　疑問文

is, am, are を be 動詞と呼び，平叙文の主語と be 動詞の位置を入れ替えて「be 動詞＋主語〜？」の形で疑問文を作ります。それ以外の一般動詞は「**Do / Does**＋主語＋動詞〜？」の形で疑問文を作ります。

例：Are you his nurse today?「あなたは今日の彼の担当看護師ですか？」
例：Do you work on weekends?「週末に仕事をしていますか？」

Exercise　次の日本語を英語に直しましょう。

1. これはあなたのかばんですか？

　　..

2. 看護師たちはあなたに親切ですか？

　　..

3

D Patient Communication

 03

❶ 音声をよく聞き，空欄に正しい英単語を入れましょう。

Healthcare Worker: Good afternoon.

Patient: Good afternoon. I'd like to see a doctor.

Healthcare Worker: Is this your first [1](   ) to this hospital?

Patient: Yes, it is. This hospital is near my hotel.

Healthcare Worker: I see. Do you have a Japanese [2](   ) insurance* card?

Patient: No, but I have overseas [3](   ) insurance. Here is my card.

Healthcare Worker: Thank you. Please fill out this [4](   ) [5](   ). We have an English version.

Patient: OK. Thank you.

> **notes**
> 医療制度は国ごとに異なります。日本国民は全員が公的な健康保険に加入していますが，アメリカでは多くの現役世代が公的保険の対象外のため，無保険者も多く，格差が見られます。

❷ 以下のステップに沿って，患者さんとの英語コミュニケーションの練習をしましょう。

Step 1. 音声に続いて会話練習（リピーティング）をしましょう。

Step 2. 先ほどのダイアローグに沿って，ペアで英語コミュニケーションの練習をしましょう。

E Reading Comprehension

❶ 英文を読んで，設問の内容が正しい場合は T，誤っている場合は F を選びましょう。

Three Key Points for Foreign Patient Care

When foreign patients come to Japanese hospitals, healthcare workers should consider three important points:

1. *Language*
Most foreign patients do not speak Japanese. Healthcare workers should be familiar with basic English phrases. Also, they should prepare patient forms in different languages.

2. *Culture*
Healthcare workers need to understand cultural differences. For example, Muslim* patients avoid pork and alcohol. This is important because healthcare workers cannot use alcohol for disinfection*.

3. *System*
Foreign travelers are not covered by Japan's National Health Insurance*. So healthcare workers should confirm whether they have overseas travel insurance.

notes　Muslim / イスラム教の，disinfection / 消毒，
Japan's National Health Insurance / 日本の国民健康保険

1. Healthcare workers do not need to learn English, because they can use patient forms in different languages.　　　　　　　　[T / F]
2. Muslim patients may refuse disinfection by alcohol.　　　[T / F]
3. Foreign travelers in Japan are automatically supported by Japan's National Health Insurance.　　　　　　　　　　　　　　　　　[T / F]

❷ 以下の Healthcare Worker の発言は上の英文の 1. language，2. culture，あるいは 3. system のどれに当てはまるか考えましょう。

1. "Do you have a Japanese medical insurance card?"　　(　　)
2. "Please fill out this English patient form."　　　　　　　(　　)
3. "Can I use alcohol for disinfection?"　　　　　　　　　(　　)

F Role Play

以下の2つのシーンで患者さんが病院の窓口で用件を伝えています。例を参考にして，今まで学習した表現を使って英語コミュニケーションの練習をしましょう。

Scene 1

(Example) see a doctor

Healthcare Worker: Good afternoon.
Patient: Good afternoon. I'd like to see a doctor.
Healthcare Worker: Is this your first visit to this hospital?
Patient: Yes, it is.
Healthcare Worker: I see. Please fill out this patient form.
Patient: Thank you.

Scene 2

receive a drug

✏ memo

....
....
....
....

臨床現場からのメッセージ1 「スマホ翻訳は使えるの？？」

私は看護師ですが，外国人患者さんの対応にスマホを使っていますよ。どちらかと言うと，こちらの言いたいことを伝えるよりも，患者さんにスマホを渡して，**言いたいことを入力してもらう**ことが多いです。

私は作業療法士ですが，**スマホの翻訳は使っていません**。なぜなら翻訳された内容が100%あっているかどうかが分からないからです。そもそもリハビリをしている時は両手がふさがっているので，スマホを操作できません。同僚の看護師や技師の間でも**賛否はわかれます**。スマホ操作に思いのほか時間がかかってしまい，結局，医療処置の時間が遅れてしまうことがあるそうです。また意図した翻訳にならない時はやり直し作業が必要になり，やはり手間がかかってしまい，だんだん必要最低限しか話さなくなってしまうという弊害もあるそうです。スマホの使用をやめて，**手書きのカードでの指さし会話に戻っている**スタッフもいるようです。**自分の言葉で話せるのが一番**だと感じました。

UNIT 2

What's the matter with you?

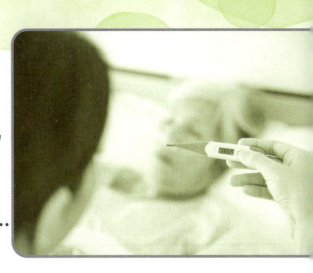

A Warm Up

総合病院には内科をはじめ，色々な診療科があります。では，具体的にどのような科があるか分かりますか？ペアで考えましょう。

B Vocabulary

04

以下の英単語の意味を選択肢の日本語を記号で選びましょう。

1. headache　[　]　2. fever　[　]　3. department　[　]
4. collect　[　]　5. recommend　[　]　6. combine　[　]

選択肢

a. 組み合わせる　b. 熱　c. 勧める　d. 頭痛　e. 〜科　f. 集める

Pronunciation Box

[k] と [g]

headache, collect, recommend や combine に [k] の発音が含まれています。[g] との違いに注意して丁寧に発音しましょう。

[k]：無声音なので，舌の付け根を上あごの後ろ部分に少しつけながら息を吐き出して発音します。

[g]：有声音なので，[k] の発音のまま喉を震わせて音を出します。

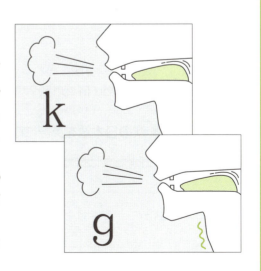

C Useful Expressions for Patient Communication

以下は患者さんとの英語コミュニケーションでよく使用される表現です。正しい意味を選択肢から選びましょう。

Healthcare Worker の表現

1. What's the matter with you? [ ]
2. Do you have a fever? [ ]
3. I recommend seeing ～ department. [ ]

Patient の表現

4. I have a headache. [ ]
5. Which department should I go to? [ ]

選択肢

a. 熱はありますか？
b. どの科に行けばいいですか？
c. どうされましたか？
d. ～科の受診をお勧めします。
e. 頭痛がします。

Grammar Box　　疑問詞 1

疑問詞を使った疑問文は「疑問詞 + be 動詞 + 主語～?」あるいは「疑問詞 + do・does + 主語 + 動詞～?」の形になります。

- what「何」　　　　　例：What is that?「あれは何ですか？」
- which「どれ」「どちら」　例：Which is your car?「あなたの車はどれですか？」
- who「だれ」　　　　例：Who is that girl?「あの少女はだれですか？」
  「だれを」「だれに」　例：Who do you work for?
  　　　　　　　　　　　「あなたは誰のために働いていますか？」
- whose「だれの」　　　例：Whose is it?「それはだれのですか？」

特に what は患者さんの容態を尋ねるときに使われます。
例：What brought you in today?「今日はどうされましたか？」

Exercise　次の日本語を英語に直しましょう。

1. あなたの好きな色は何ですか？

　　..

2. ナースステーションはどこですか？

　　..

• Unit 2 • What's the matter with you?

D Patient Communication

 05

❶ 音声をよく聞き，空欄に正しい英単語を入れましょう。

Healthcare Worker: Hello. What's the ¹(　　　　) with you?

Patient: Hello. I have a ²(　　　　) from last night.

Healthcare Worker: OK. Do you have a ³(　　　　)?

Patient: Yes. 100.4° Fahrenheit*.

Healthcare Worker: Well, that's 38.0° Celsius. I see.

Patient: Which ⁴(　　　　) should I go to?

Healthcare Worker: I ⁵(　　　　) seeing the internal medicine department.*

Patient: Thank you very much.

> **notes**
> **Fahrenheit**（°F）は主にアメリカで使われる温度の表記方法です。日本をはじめ世界的には Celsius（℃）が一般的です。100°Fが約37.8℃であることを知っておけば便利です。
> **the internal medicine department** 内科

❷ 以下のステップに沿って，患者さんとの英語コミュニケーションの練習をしましょう。

Step 1. 音声に続いて会話練習（リピーティング）をしましょう。

Step 2. 先ほどのダイアローグに沿って，ペアで英語コミュニケーションの練習をしましょう。

E Reading Comprehension

❶ 英文を読んで，設問の内容が正しい場合はT，誤っている場合はFを選びましょう。

Effective Patient Interview Techniques

Collecting information from patients is important. Healthcare workers can use two types of questions during interviews*.

*Closed-ended questions**

"Do you have a fever?" or "Do you have a headache?" are examples of closed-ended questions. Healthcare workers can get quick answers. But the problem is that patients might answer the questions with only "yes" or "no." In this case, they cannot get detailed information.

*Open-ended questions**

"How are you feeling?" is an example of an open-ended question. These questions help healthcare workers get more detailed information. But sometimes, patients might give short answers such as "nothing special,"* or "I'm OK."

So, healthcare workers should choose or combine these two types of questions for collecting information.

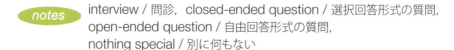

notes interview / 問診，closed-ended question / 選択回答形式の質問，
open-ended question / 自由回答形式の質問，
nothing special / 別に何もない

1. Closed-ended questions allow patients to provide detailed information.　[T / F]
2. Healthcare workers can get basic information from open-ended questions.　[T / F]
3. Healthcare workers should only use open-ended questions for information collection.　[T / F]

❷ 以下のHealthcare Workerの発言は上の英文の "closed-ended question" あるいは "open-ended question" のどちらに当てはまるか考えましょう。

1. "What's the matter with you?"　　　　　　　　　　　　　　(　　　)
2. "Are you feeling better today?"　　　　　　　　　　　　　　(　　　)
3. "Could you tell me about your headache?"　　　　　　　　(　　　)

• Unit 2 • What's the matter with you?

F Role Play

以下の２つのシーンで患者さんがある症状を伝えています。例を参考にして，今まで学習した表現を使って英語コミュニケーションの練習をしましょう。

Scene 1

(Example)
cough

Healthcare Worker: Hello. What's the matter with you?
Patient: Hello. I have a cough from last night.
Healthcare Worker: OK. Do you have a fever?
Patient: No, I don't.
Healthcare Worker: I recommend seeing the internal medicine department.
Patient: Thank you.

Scene 2

nausea

✏ memo

....
....
....
....
....
....

| 臨床現場からのメッセージ２ | 「発熱しても病気じゃない？」 |

　　　　在宅訪問の時は体温，咳，鼻水の有無など，色々な確認事項があります。高齢で寝たきりの方の場合，他に自覚症状がなくても，体温が38度近くある場合があります。これは**「こもり熱」**といって，布団の中に熱がこもって体温が上がっている状態です。この場合は，服に空気を入れたり，布団をバサバサと動かして熱を逃がすことで，すぐに熱を下げることができます。検温の数値も大事ですが，**患者さんと話しながら容態を把握**することも大事です。外国人患者さんには，どうしても最低限の情報伝達だけになってしまいがちなので注意しましょう。

UNIT 3
I'm going to take a blood sample

A Warm Up

みなさんも病院や健康診断などで採血をされた経験があるでしょう。採血時の医療従事者と患者さんの会話はどのようなものでしょうか？ペアで考えましょう。

B Vocabulary

06

以下の英単語の意味を選択肢の日本語を記号で選びましょう。

1. fist　　　　　[　　]　2. thumb　　　　　　　　[　　]　3. skin trouble　[　　]
4. alcohol wipe　[　　]　5. take a blood sample　[　　]　6. roll up　　　[　　]

選択肢
a. 親指　　b. こぶし　　c. アルコールティッシュ　　d. まくる　　e. 採血する　　f. 肌荒れ

Pronunciation Box

[θ] と [ð]

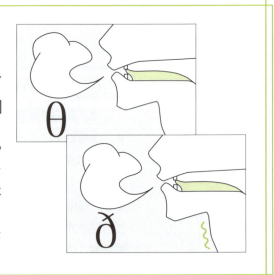

thumbに[θ]の発音が含まれています。[ð]との違いに注意して丁寧に発音しましょう。
[θ]：無声音なので，上の前歯に舌先をつけ，前歯でその舌先を挟み，そこから息を吐き出して発音します。日本語の「ス」とは全く違う音なので注意しましょう。
[ð]：有声音なので，[θ]の発音のまま喉を震わせて音を出します。

• Unit 3 • I'm going to take a blood sample

C Useful Expressions for Patient Communication

以下は患者さんとの英語コミュニケーションでよく使用される表現です。正しい意味を選択肢から選びましょう。

Healthcare Worker の表現

1. May I confirm your name and date of birth? [ ]
2. Have you ever had skin trouble with alcohol wipes? [ ]
3. I'm going to take a blood sample. [ ]
4. Roll up your sleeve. [ ]
5. Make a fist with your thumb inside. [ ]
6. It may sting a little. [ ]

Patient の表現

7. My date of birth is 〜. [ ]
8. No, I haven't. [ ]
9. OK. Like this? [ ]

選択肢

a. 私の生年月日は〜です。
b. 少しチクッとするかもしれません。
c. これから採血します。
d. わかりました。こうですか？
e. いいえ，ありません。
f. 袖をまくってください。
g. お名前と生年月日を確認させていただけますか？
h. 親指を中に入れてこぶしを作ってください。
i. 今までにアルコールティッシュで皮膚が荒れたことはありますか？

Grammar Box　　　未来形 1 (be going to〜)

未来を表す表現に「**be going to** ＋動詞の原形」があり，「これから〜するつもりだ」「〜する予定だ」という意味になります。これから行う治療や検査などを患者さんに説明する際に使用されます。

例：I am going to take your temperature.「これから検温を行います。」

Exercise　次の日本語を英語に直しましょう。

1. 私達は放課後に勉強するつもりです。

　　..

2. これからレントゲン（**an X-ray**）を撮ります。

　　..

13

D Patient Communication

 07

❶ 音声をよく聞き，以下のスクリプトの空欄に正しい英単語を入れましょう。

Healthcare Worker: Good morning. May I ¹(　　　　) your name and date of birth?

Patient: Good morning. Yes, I'm John White. My date of birth is January 15th, 2006.

Healthcare Worker: Thank you, Mr. White. Have you ever had ²(　　　　) ³(　　　　) with alcohol wipes*?

Patient: No, I haven't.

Healthcare Worker: OK. I'm going to take a blood sample.

Patient: OK. That's fine.

Healthcare Worker: Roll up your sleeve. Make a fist with your ⁴(　　　　) inside.

Patient: OK. Like this?

Healthcare Worker: That's right. It may ⁵(　　　　) a little. …. We've finished. You can relax now.

Patient: Thank you.

> **notes**
> 採血時に注意するアレルギーとして，アルコール以外にもゴム製品へのアレルギーであるラテックス・アレルギー（latex allergies）もあります。

❷ 以下のステップに沿って，患者さんとの英語コミュニケーションの練習をしましょう。

Step 1. 音声に続いて会話練習（リピーティング）をしましょう。

Step 2. 先ほどのダイアローグに沿って，ペアで英語コミュニケーションの練習をしましょう。

E Reading Comprehension

❶ 英文を読んで，設問の内容が正しい場合は T，誤っている場合は F を選びましょう。

Communication Techniques for Blood Draws

Some people don't like blood draws* because they fear needles*. For these patients, communication is important. First, ask them if they're scared*. By talking to them, you can understand their discomfort level*. Don't use the needle until they say OK. This takes more time, but you should be patient. Then, watch their face carefully during the blood draw. Talking to them is a good way to relax them. You can advise them to take deep breaths*. It can ease pain. By following these tips, patients will feel more relaxed during blood draws.

notes blood draw / 採血，needle / 針，scared / 怖がる，
discomfort level / 不快度，deep breath / 深呼吸

1. During a blood draw, you should focus only on the needle. [T / F]
2. Taking deep breaths during a blood draw is not effective in decreasing pain. [T / F]
3. Communication is important to relax patients who fear needles. [T / F]

❷ 以下の Healthcare Worker の発言は上の英文の "understand discomfort level"，"relax patients"，あるいは "give advice" のどれに当てはまるか考えましょう。

1. "It may sting a little, but don't worry."   (   )
2. "Have you ever felt sick during a blood draw?"   (   )
3. "What's your hobby? Tell me about it."   (   )

F Role Play

以下の2つのシーンは採血の事前確認の場面です。例を参考にして，今まで学習した表現を使って英語コミュニケーションの練習をしましょう。なお Scene 2 の Patient はあなた自身という設定で会話しましょう。

Scene 1 (Example) John White

Healthcare Worker: Good morning. May I confirm your name and date of birth?

Patient: Good morning. Yes, I'm John White. My date of birth is January 15th, 2006.

Healthcare Worker: Thank you, Mr. White. Have you ever had skin trouble with alcohol wipes?

Patient: No, I haven't.

Healthcare Worker: OK. I'm going to take a blood sample.

Patient: All right.

✏ memo
....
....
....
....
....

Scene 2 You

臨床現場からのメッセージ3 「採血は苦手」

　採血が苦手な患者さんは結構います。そのような患者さんには「顔をそむけてください」とか「見ないでください」などと言います。また，「今から～します」と言うと，逆に患者さんがぐっと力を入れて身構えてしまい，逆効果になることがあります。そのため，「採血は苦手ですか。そうですか，大丈夫ですよ，リラックスしてください」と言いながら，さっと針を入れてしまいます。

　声掛けが大事なのは日本人でも外国人でも変わりません。外国人患者さんだからといって，**無言で採血するのは NG** です。簡単な表現でもよいので，**自分の言葉でコミュニケーションを取る**ことで，患者さんに安心感を与え，信頼関係を築くことができます。

UNIT 4
Let me explain our daily routine

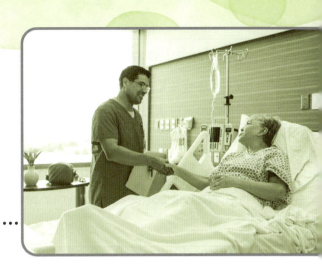

A Warm Up

入院患者さんがやってきたら，まず看護師などの医療従事者が1日の流れを説明します。では，具体的にどのような点を説明すれば良いでしょうか？また病室にある備品の説明も必要です。どのような備品や設備が病室にあるでしょうか？ペアで考えましょう。

B Vocabulary 08

以下の英単語の意味を選択肢の日本語を記号で選びましょう。

1. explain   [   ]   2. daily routine   [   ]   3. temperature   [   ]
4. examination   [   ]   5. be familiar with 〜 [   ]   6. go outside   [   ]

選択肢
a. 日課・1日の流れ   b. 検査   c. 体温   d. 〜に慣れている   e. 外出する   f. 説明する

Pronunciation Box

[u] と [u:]

daily routine に [u:] の発音が含まれています。[u] との違いに注意して丁寧に発音しましょう。

[u]：日本語の「ウ」よりも「オ」のように広くします。舌の最も高い部分と上あごの空間を狭め，唇を丸い形にして「ウ」と発音します。

[u:]：[u] と同じ方法で，音を伸ばして発音します。

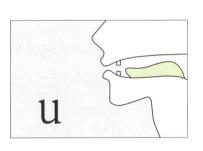

C Useful Expressions for Patient Communication

以下は患者さんとの英語コミュニケーションでよく使用される表現です。正しい意味を選択肢から選びましょう。

Healthcare Worker の表現

1. Let me explain our daily routine. [ ]
2. We will come to take your temperature at.... [ ]
3. The doctor will come soon. [ ]
4. The doctor will explain the examination. [ ]

Patient の表現

5. What time does the examination start? [ ]
6. Can I talk with the doctor today? [ ]

選択肢

a. 先生（医師）と今日話すことはできますか？
b. 〜時に体温を測りに来ます。
c. 1日の流れを説明します。
d. 先生（医師）から検査について説明があります。
e. 検査は何時に始まりますか？
f. 先生（医師）はまもなく来られます。

Grammar Box　　　未来形 2 (will)

Unit 3 で学習した「be going to + 動詞の原形」以外にも，未来を表す表現に「will + 動詞の原形」があり，「〜するだろう」「〜するつもりだ」という意味になります。

例：We will come to take your temperature around 6:30.
　　「6:30 に検温に伺うつもりです。」

Exercise　次の日本語を英語に直しましょう。

1. 彼は明日病院に行くだろう。

　　　　　　　　　　　　　　　　　　　　　　

2. 看護師がまもなく採血に来るだろう。

• Unit 4 • Let me explain our daily routine

D Patient Communication

 09

❶ 音声をよく聞き，以下のスクリプトの空欄に正しい英単語を入れましょう。

Healthcare Worker: Let me explain our ¹(　　　　) ²(　　　　). We'll come to take your ³(　　　　) around 6:30 in the morning.

Patient: OK. So I have to wake up early.

Healthcare Worker: Yes. The wake-up time is 6 am and the lights-out time* is 10 at night.

Patient: What time is breakfast?

Healthcare Worker: At 7 am. You'll have lunch at noon and dinner at 6 pm.

Patient: Can I ⁴(　　　　) with the doctor today?

Healthcare Worker: Of course. The doctor will come soon.

Patient: What time does the ⁵(　　　　) start?

Healthcare Worker: The doctor will explain it.

Patient: I see. Thank you very much.

> notes
> lights-out time 消灯時間

❷ 以下のステップに沿って，患者さんとの英語コミュニケーションの練習をしましょう。

Step 1. 音声に続いて会話練習（リピーティング）をしましょう。

Step 2. 先ほどのダイアローグに沿って，ペアで英語コミュニケーションの練習をしましょう。

19

E Reading Comprehension

❶ 英文を読んで，設問の内容が正しい場合は T，誤っている場合は F を選びましょう。

Understanding Hospital Rules

Patients need to follow some rules in Japanese hospitals. But foreign patients are sometimes not familiar with these rules.

Permission for going outside
Patients cannot leave the hospital without permission*. But in some other countries, patients can go outside freely. Patients from such countries may go out without permission because they are not aware of this rule.

Explaining visiting hours
There are specific visiting hours* in Japanese hospitals. But some foreign patients are surprised at this rule because they can visit their family anytime in their home countries. Patients from such countries may get confused* because they can't see their family whenever they want to.

Hospital rules are different in each country. Healthcare workers should understand cultural differences and carefully explain the rules to foreign patients.

notes without permission / 無断で，
visiting hours / 面会時間，get confused / 混乱する

1. Hospital rules are similar among various countries.　　　　　　　[T / F]
2. Visiting hours in Japanese hospitals are flexible, so foreign patients can visit their families at any time.　　　　　　　[T / F]
3. Healthcare workers should consider cultural differences and explain hospital rules to foreign patients.　　　　　　　[T / F]

❷ 以下の Healthcare Worker の発言は上の英文の "permission for going outside" あるいは "explaining visiting hours" のどれに当てはまる内容か考えましょう。

1. "You should check the visiting hours beforehand." (　　　　　　　)
2. "Did you receive approval from the doctor to go outside the hospital?"
　　　　　　　(　　　　　　　)

• Unit 4 • Let me explain our daily routine

F Role Play

以下の２つのシーンで医療従事者が患者さんに入院生活の流れを説明しています。例を参考にして，今まで学習した表現を使って英語コミュニケーションの練習をしましょう。

Healthcare Worker: Let me explain our daily routine. We'll come to take your temperature around 6:30 in the morning.

Patient: OK. So I have to wake up early.

Healthcare Worker: Yes. The wake-up time is 6 am and the lights-out time is 10 pm.

Patient: Can I talk with the doctor today?

Healthcare Worker: Of course. The doctor will come to see you at 11 o'clock.

Patient: Thank you.

✎ memo
....
....
....
....

| 臨床現場からのメッセージ４ | 「入院ルールを守ること」 |

　入院生活にはルールがありますが，そのルールを守れない患者さんもいます。呼吸器疾患にもかかわらず禁煙できない患者さんなど，制限のかかる病気の場合，どうしても患者さんがストレスを感じます。患者さんの話を聞くなどして，**ストレスを発散させてあげる**ことが大事です。

　また外国人の患者さんの場合，病気だけでなく**文化や言葉の違いが**ストレスの原因になるケースもあるので，患者さんやご家族ともコミュニケーションをとり，**病院のルールに納得してもらう**ことが大事だと思います。

UNIT 5
I'm going to ask you about your lifestyle habits

A Warm Up

患者さんの生活習慣を把握することは治療計画を立てる上で非常に重要です。患者さんが快適な入院生活を過ごすうえで，生活習慣や時に宗教について医療従事者は何を把握する必要があるでしょうか？ペアで考えましょう。

B Vocabulary

CD 10

以下の英単語の意味を選択肢の日本語を記号で選びましょう。

1. quit　　　[　]
2. exclude　　[　]
3. habit　　　　　　[　]
4. belief　　[　]
5. respect　　[　]
6. religious restriction　[　]

選択肢
a. やめる　　b. 宗教上の制限　　c. 敬意を払う　　d. 除外する　　e. 習慣　　f. 信念

Pronunciation Box

[l] と [r]

exclude, belief, respect や religious restriction に [l] と [r] の発音が含まれています。日本語のラ行の音とは異なるので気をつけましょう。
[r]：舌を根元から後ろに巻き込み，舌先をどこにもつけずに発音します。
[l]：舌先を前歯の裏近くまで前に持っていき，上の歯茎につけたまま発音します。

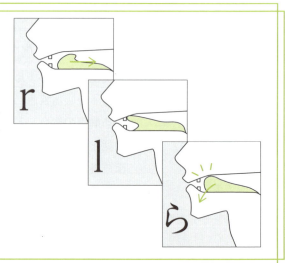

• Unit 5 • I'm going to ask you about your lifestyle habits

C Useful Expressions for Patient Communication

以下は患者さんとの英語コミュニケーションでよく使用される表現です。正しい意味を選択肢から選びましょう。

Healthcare Worker の表現

1. I'm going to ask you about your lifestyle habits. [ ]
2. Do you smoke? [ ]
3. Are there any other religious restrictions? [ ]
4. Feel free to ask anytime. [ ]

Patient の表現

5. I used to smoke but I quit. [ ]
6. I don't eat pork for religious reasons. [ ]
7. Can you exclude pork from my meals? [ ]

選択肢
a. 宗教上の理由で豚肉を食べません。
b. 豚肉を食事から除外できますか？
c. あなたの生活習慣についてお聞きします。
d. 喫煙をされますか？
e. いつでも遠慮なく聞いてください。
f. 以前は喫煙をしていましたが，やめました。
g. 他に宗教上の制限はありますか？

Grammar Box　　現在形・過去形

現在形は「現在の状態」あるいは「現在の習慣」を表します。
例：The shop opens at 9 o'clock every day.「その店は毎日 9 時に開店します。」

過去形は「過去に起こったこと」を表します。be 動詞は am・is → was，are → were の形にします。一般動詞は語尾に -ed をつける場合と不規則に変化する場合があります。
例：I watched a movie last night.「私は昨晩映画を見ました。」
また「主語 + **used to** + **動詞の原形**」で「以前は〜だった」という意味になります。
例：I used to smoke.「以前はタバコをすっていました。」

Exercise 次の日本語を英語に直しましょう。

1. 私は毎日音楽を聴いています。

2. 以前，私の父はお酒を飲んでいました。

23

D Patient Communication

❶ 音声をよく聞き，以下のスクリプトの空欄に正しい英単語を入れましょう。

Healthcare Worker: I'm going to ask you about your lifestyle ¹(   ). Do you smoke?

Patient: No, I don't. I used to smoke but I ²(   ) 10 years ago.

Healthcare Worker: I see. I heard you don't eat any pork.

Patient: That's right. I don't eat pork for religious reasons*. Can you ³(   ) pork from my meals?

Healthcare Worker: Yes. I'll tell our kitchen staff. Are there any other religious ⁴(   )?

Patient: No, that's all.

Healthcare Worker: OK. If you have any questions, feel ⁵(   ) to ask anytime.

Patient: Thank you.

> *notes*
> 宗教と食事の関係は深く，例えばイスラム教では豚肉やアルコールが禁止されています。また多くのヒンドゥ教徒は採食主義者（vegetarian）で，特に牛肉が禁止されています。最近では，完全菜食主義者（vegan）といった，動物福祉，環境保護あるいは健康の観点から，あらゆる動物性食品の摂取を避ける人も増えています。

❷ 以下のステップに沿って，患者さんとの英語コミュニケーションの練習をしましょう。

Step 1. 音声に続いて会話練習（リピーティング）をしましょう。

Step 2. 先ほどのダイアローグに沿って，ペアで英語コミュニケーションの練習をしましょう。

• Unit 5 • I'm going to ask you about your lifestyle habits

E Reading Comprehension

❶ 英文を読んで，設問の内容が正しい場合は T，誤っている場合は F を選びましょう。

Understanding Vegetarians

Some foreign patients might be vegetarians. What is a vegetarian? Vegetarians eat food only from plants such as nuts, fruits, grains*, and vegetables. They do not eat meat.

Types of vegetarians
There are about 10 types of vegetarians. They differ based on their beliefs and cultures. Some vegetarians eat honey, eggs, milk, or even fish. Others eat only fruits and nuts but do not eat vegetables.

Why
Why do people become vegetarians? Some vegetarians care about animals and don't want to eat them. Others become vegetarians for their health. In India, about one-third of the people don't eat meat because it's part of their culture.

If a patient is a vegetarian, healthcare workers should ask them what they can eat. Healthcare workers should respect their choices and cultural beliefs.

notes   grain / 穀物

1. Most foreign patients are vegetarian.   [T / F]
2. Every vegetarian avoids eating fish.   [T / F]
3. The main reason many Indians are vegetarian is because they care about animals.   [T / F]

❷ 本文の内容を踏まえ，空欄に入る適切な Healthcare Worker の発言を選択肢から選びましょう。

Healthcare Worker: Do you have any dietary restrictions that I should be aware of?"

Patient: Actually, I'm a vegetarian. I don't eat meat.

Healthcare Worker: (1   )

選択肢

a. Oh, that's too bad. Animal protein is important for human body.

b. Thank you for letting me know. We'll avoid meat.

c. I see. Maybe you should try some meat. It's good for your health.

25

F Role Play

以下の2つのシーンで医療従事者が患者さんに生活習慣に関する質問をしています。例を参考にして，今まで学習した表現を使って英語コミュニケーションの練習をしましょう。

Scene 1
(Example) Muslim

Healthcare Worker: I'm going to ask you about your lifestyle habits. Do you drink alcohol?
Patient: No, I don't.
Healthcare Worker: I see. I heard you don't eat any pork.
Patient: That's right. I don't eat pork for religious reasons.
Healthcare Worker: OK. If you have any questions, feel free to ask anytime.

Scene 2
vegetarian

✏️ memo
....
....
....
....
....
....

臨床現場からのメッセージ5 ｜ 「宗教と輸血の関係」

患者さんの中には**宗教上の理由から輸血や採血を拒否される方**がいます。そのため，医療機関ごとにガイドラインがあり，どのような事態でも輸血しない**「絶対的無輸血」**や，可能な限り輸血はしないが，救命のために輸血以外の方法が無い場合のみ輸血を行う**「相対的無輸血」**などの方針があります。実際の現場でそのような患者さんがいれば，まずは**医師に相談**し対応をお願いします。

UNIT 6
Have you had any surgeries before?

A Warm Up

これまでかかった病気（既往歴）やご家族の病歴を患者さんに尋ねることは非常に重要です。では，なぜこれらの情報が重要なのでしょうか？ペアで考えましょう。

B Vocabulary

以下の英単語の意味を選択肢の日本語を記号で選びましょう。

1. surgery   [   ]   2. cooperation   [   ]   3. heart   [   ]
4. past   [   ]   5. unrelated   [   ]   6. be related to ～   [   ]

選択肢
a. 協力   b. ～に関連している   c. 無関係な   d. 心臓   e. 過去の   f. 手術

Pronunciation Box

[ə], [ɜː], [e]

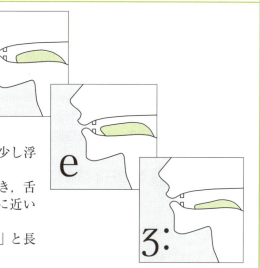

surgery に [ɜː]（əː）の発音が含まれています。[ə]や[e]との違いに注意して丁寧に発音しましょう。

[ə]：口全体の力を抜いて，舌を下あごから少し浮かせた状態で短く「ア」と発音します。

[e]：口を自然と開きながら唇を横に少し引き，舌を口の中央に置いた状態で日本語の「エ」に近い発音をします。

[ɜː]：[ə]よりも舌を少し下に置いて「アー」と長めに発音します。

C Useful Expressions for Patient Communication

以下は患者さんとの英語コミュニケーションでよく使用される表現です。正しい意味を選択肢から選びましょう。

Healthcare Worker の表現

1. Have you had any surgeries before? [ ]
2. Do you remember when it was? [ ]
3. How about your parents? [ ]
4. Thank you for your cooperation. [ ]

Patient の表現

5. I have had surgery for heart disease. [ ]
6. I think it was three years ago. [ ]
7. My grandfather died of a heart attack. [ ]

選択肢

a. 心臓病の手術を受けたことがあります。
b. 以前に手術を受けたことはありますか？
c. 祖父が心臓発作で亡くなりました。
d. ご協力ありがとうございました。
e. ご両親はどうですか？
f. それがいつか覚えていますか？
g. 3年前だったと思います。

Grammar Box　　現在完了形

現在完了形（「**have / has ＋過去分詞**」）は過去から現在までの期間に起こったことについて述べます。主に3つの代表的な使い方があります。

1. 継続「（今も）〜している」
　例：I have lived in Japan for three years.「私は日本に3年間住んでいます。」
2. 完了「〜してしまった」例：I have lost my key.「私は鍵をなくしてしまった。」
3. 経験「〜したことがある」
　例：She has visited many countries.「彼女は多くの国を訪れたことがあります。」

医療従事者が使用する機会が多いのは，3．の経験の用法で，Have you had any surgeries before? のような疑問文で患者さんの過去の病歴を問えます。

Exercise　次の日本語を英語に直しましょう。

1. 私はちょうど部屋の掃除が終わったところです。

　_____

2. 私は以前にこの病院に来たことがあります。

　_____

D Patient Communication

❶ 音声をよく聞き，空欄に正しい英単語を入れましょう。

Healthcare Worker: Have you had any ¹(   ) before?

Patient: Yes, I've had surgery for heart disease.

Healthcare Worker: I see. Do you ²(   ) when it was?

Patient: I think it was five years ago.

Healthcare Worker: OK. Thank you. Then, how about your parents or siblings*?

Patient: Well, my grandfather ³(   ) ⁴(   ) a heart attack.

Healthcare Worker: I see. Thank you for your ⁵(   ). It's important for us to understand your family health history.

> **notes**
> sibling（男女の区別なく使用される）きょうだい。性別や出生順に関係なく，同じ親から生まれた兄，弟，姉または妹を差します。

❷ 以下のステップに沿って，患者さんとの英語コミュニケーションの練習をしましょう。

Step 1. 音声に続いて会話練習（リピーティング）をしましょう。

Step 2. 先ほどのダイアローグに沿って，ペアで英語コミュニケーションの練習をしましょう。

E Reading Comprehension

❶ 英文を読んで，設問の内容が正しい場合は T，誤っている場合は F を選びましょう。

The Importance of Patients' Past Illnesses

Healthcare workers need to know patients' past illnesses. Patients may think past illnesses are unrelated. But this information is important for patient care.

Medical history

Healthcare workers need to get detailed information about patients' past illnesses, accidents, hospitalizations*, and surgeries. Childhood illnesses, accidents and operations* are also important. They may be related to the current* disease.

Family health history

Family health history is a record of the diseases and health conditions in your family. Healthcare workers need to collect family history information because many illnesses are related to genetics*.

 notes　hospitalization / 入院，operation / 手術，
current / 現在の，genetics / 遺伝的特徴

1. Past illnesses are unrelated to patient care.　　　　　　　　　[T / F]
2. Childhood illnesses could be relevant to the current health condition.
　　　　　　　　　　　　　　　　　　　　　　　　　　　　　[T / F]
3. Healthcare workers should understand patients' genetic conditions.
　　　　　　　　　　　　　　　　　　　　　　　　　　　　　[T / F]

❷ 以下の Healthcare Worker の発言は上の英文の "Medical history" あるいは "Family health history" のどちらに関する質問か考えましょう。

1. "Have these symptoms happened before?" (　　　　　　　　　　)
2. "Does any member of your family have the same illness?"
　　　　　　　　　　　　　　　　　　　　　　　(　　　　　　　　　　)

• Unit 6 • Have you had any surgeries before?

F Role Play

以下の２つのシーンで医療従事者と患者さんが過去の病歴について話をしています。例を参考にして，今まで学習した表現を使って英語コミュニケーションの練習をしましょう。

Scene 1

(Example)
diabetes

Healthcare Worker: Have you had any serious diseases before?
Patient: Yes, I have diabetes.
Healthcare Worker: I see. Do you remember when it started?
Patient: I think it was three years ago.
Healthcare Worker: I see. Thank you for your cooperation.

Scene 2

lung cancer
(two years ago, surgery)

✏ memo

....
....
....
....
....
....
....

臨床現場からのメッセージ 6 | 「健康相談はよくある」

病歴を確認する際に，**患者さんから健康相談をされることはよくあります**。例えば，「前に手術をしたけど，時々ここがしびれるの。どうしたらいい？」のような相談です。患者さんにとって医師よりも看護師や技師の方が話しやすいのかもしれません。ただ，患者さんがその手術について病院に申告をしておらず，こちらの記録にない場合もあります。その場合は「どんな手術をしたのですか？」などと質問をして，情報を引き出すようにしています。一問一答ではなく，**対話しながら情報を引き出す**ことが大事ですね。

31

UNIT 7

Do you have any allergies?

A Warm Up

アレルギーを引き起こす物質を「アレルゲン」と言います。では，どのようなアレルゲンがありますか？また臨床現場で必ず把握しておくべきアレルゲンは何でしょうか？ペアで考えましょう。

B Vocabulary

CD 14

以下の英単語の意味を選択肢の日本語を記号で選びましょう。

1. allergy [　]　　2. allergic reaction [　]　　3. breathing [　]
4. avoid [　]　　5. inform [　]　　6. have difficulty in ～ [　]

選択肢

a. 呼吸　　b. 知らせる　　c. 避ける　　d. アレルギー　　e. アレルギー反応　　f. ～が難しい

Pronunciation Box

[i] と [iː]

informやhave difficulty in～に [i] の発音が含まれています。[iː] との違いに注意して丁寧に発音しましょう。
[i]：日本語の「イ」ほど口を横に開かず，力を抜いた状態で「イ」と発音します。舌と上あごとの空間をできるだけ狭くし，口の前方部分に舌先を置いて発音します。
[iː]：[i] と同じ方法で，音を伸ばして発音します。

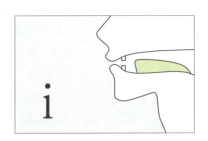

• Unit 7 • Do you have any allergies?

C Useful Expressions for Patient Communication

以下は患者さんとの英語コミュニケーションでよく使用される表現です。正しい意味を選択肢から選びましょう。

Healthcare Worker の表現

1. Do you have any allergies? [　]
2. Can you tell me more about that? [　]
3. We'll make sure to avoid ～. [　]

Patient の表現

4. I have an allergy to nuts. [　]
5. I had an allergic reaction. [　]
6. I had difficulty in breathing. [　]

選択肢

a. 私たちは～を避けるようにします。
b. それについてより詳しく教えていただけますか？
c. 息が苦しくなりました。　　d. アレルギー反応がありました。
e. ナッツにアレルギーがあります。　f. アレルギーはありますか？

Grammar Box　　　　接続詞

接続詞は文と文をつなぐ働きがあります。臨床現場でよく使用される接続詞は，時間（before「～する前に」, after「～する後に」, when「～する時に」, while「～する間に」），理由（because「～のため」），そして条件（if「もし～なら」）の3種類です。

before : Before you go to bed, remember to turn off the lights.
「寝る前にライトを消すのを忘れないでください。」
after : After her exams were over, she went traveling.
「試験が終わった後に，彼女は旅行に行きました。」
when : When it rains, I like staying home.
「雨の時は，私は家で過ごすのが好きです。」
while : While she cooks dinner, she listens to music.
「夕食を作る間，彼女は音楽を聴きます。」
because : She didn't go to school, because she had a cold.
「彼女は風邪のため学校に行きませんでした。」
if : If you need help, please ask me.
「もし助けが必要なら，私に頼んでください。」

Exercise　次の日本語を英語に直しましょう。

1. 夕食を食べる前に手を洗ってください。

2. 風邪をひいたので，明日病院に行きます。

D Patient Communication

❶ 音声をよく聞き，以下のスクリプトの空欄に正しい英単語を入れましょう。

Healthcare Worker: Good morning.

Patient: Good morning.

Healthcare Worker: Before we start, I just need to confirm some information with you. Do you have any allergies?

Patient: Yes, I have an allergy to nuts.

Healthcare Worker: OK. Can you ¹(   ) me more about that?

Patient: I had an ²(   ) ³(   ) when I was a child. I had difficulty in breathing*.

Healthcare Worker: I see. We'll make sure to ⁴(   ) nuts during your ⁵(   ) here. Thank you for confirming that with me.

> **notes**
> 軽度のアレルギー症状では鼻水（runny nose），発疹（skin rash），くしゃみ（sneezing）などがあります。重度の場合は呼吸困難（difficulty in breathing）などの命に関わる症状を引き起こすこともあります。

❷ 以下のステップに沿って，患者さんとの英語コミュニケーションの練習をしましょう。

Step 1. 音声に続いて会話練習（リピーティング）をしましょう。

Step 2. 先ほどのダイアローグに沿って，ペアで英語コミュニケーションの練習をしましょう。

• Unit 7 • Do you have any allergies?

E Reading Comprehension

❶ 英文を読んで，設問の内容が正しい場合は T，誤っている場合は F を選びましょう。

Confirming Patients' Allergies

It is important for nurses to confirm patients' allergies because allergies can cause serious problems. Nurses should be careful about several key points for patient safety:

A. Nurses should use simple language when asking about allergies.
B. Nurses should use open-ended questions because they can get detailed information from patients.
C. Nurses should confirm patients' allergies and previous allergic reactions by checking their medical records*.
D. Nurses should report patients' allergies and inform other medical team members.
E. Nurses should educate patients on how to avoid allergens* in their daily life. It is important for patients to recognize the signs of an allergic reaction and seek medical help.

notes   medical records / カルテ，allergen / アレルゲン

1. Nurses should use technical language when asking about allergies.
[T / F]
2. Nurses should try to get detailed information in allergy interviews.
[T / F]
3. Nurses only need to inform the patient's doctor about their allergies.
[T / F]

❷ 以下の Healthcare Worker の発言は上の英文の "key points" の A～E のどれに当てはまるか考えましょう。

1. "Do you have any allergies?"　　　　　　　　　　　（　　）
2. "Can you tell me more about that?"　　　　　　　　（　　）
3. "We'll check your medical records for allergies."　　（　　）

35

F Role Play

以下の2つのシーンで医療従事者が患者さんにアレルギーの有無について質問をしています。例を参考にして，今まで学習した表現を使って英語コミュニケーションの練習をしましょう。

Scene 1

(Example) egg allergy, skin rash

Healthcare Worker: Before we start, I just need to confirm some information with you. Do you have any allergies?

Patient: Yes, I have an allergy to eggs. I have a skin rash when I eat them.

Healthcare Worker: OK. Then, do you have drug allergies?

Patient: No, I don't.

Healthcare Worker: I see. Thank you for confirming that with me.

Scene 2

wheat allergy, nausea

✏️ *memo*

....
....
....
....
....

臨床現場からのメッセージ 7 ｜ 「雑談は大事」

患者さんとの雑談は大事です。悩み事や困っていることを引き出し，それに対して助言することで，患者さんとの信頼関係を築けます。また，普段の生活や体調の変化など医師には話しにくいことも，雑談から情報が得られます。食品やそれ以外のアレルギーについても，雑談から新規の情報が出てくることがあります。"How are you?" などの基礎的表現でよいので，**積極的にコミュニケーションをとることが大切**だと思います。

UNIT 8

How would you describe the pain?

A Warm Up

「傷口がズキズキする」や「頭がガンガンする」など，痛みには色々な表現があります。では，他にどのような表現があるでしょうか？ペアで考えましょう。

B Vocabulary

CD 16

以下の英単語の意味を選択肢の日本語を記号で選びましょう。

1. pain   [   ]   2. describe   [   ]   3. sharp   [   ]
4. dull   [   ]   5. rate   [   ]   6. aching   [   ]

選択肢

a. 鋭い   b. 表現する   c. うずく   d. 痛み   e. 評価する   f. 鈍い

Pronunciation Box

[s] と [z], [ʃ] と [ʒ]

describe や sharp に [s] や [ʃ] の発音が含まれています。

[s]：日本語の「サ」行に近く，唇は少しだけ開いて歯を閉じ，舌先を上の歯茎のあたりに近づけ息を吐き出し，「スー」と空気を出します。

[z]：[s] の発音のまま喉を震わせて音を出します。

[ʃ]：無声音なので，唇を日本語の「ウ」のような形で歯を閉じて，舌の前方を上の前歯の歯茎の裏のギリギリまで近づけ，「シュー」と空気が漏れるような音で発音します。

[ʒ]：[ʃ] の発音のまま喉を震わせて音を出します。

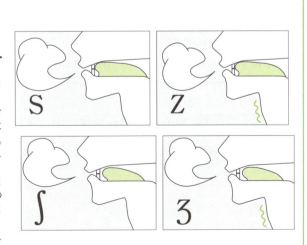

C Useful Expressions for Patient Communication

以下は患者さんとの英語コミュニケーションでよく使用される表現です。正しい意味を選択肢から選びましょう。

Healthcare Worker の表現

1. How are you feeling? [ ]
2. How would you describe your pain? [ ]
3. Is it a sharp pain? [ ]
4. How would you rate your pain? [ ]

Patient の表現

5. My knee hurt last night. [ ]
6. Not too bad. [ ]
7. I think it's a dull pain. [ ]

選択肢

a. 鋭い痛みですか？
b. あまりひどくはありません。
c. 体調はいかがですか？
d. どのような痛みですか？
e. 昨夜は膝が痛みました。
f. 痛みはどれくらいですか？
g. にぶい痛みだと思います。

Grammar Box　　疑問詞 2

Unit 2 で学習した疑問詞以外にも，when「いつ」，where「どこで」，how「どのように」，why「なぜ」があります。臨床現場では when は「いつ症状が始まったか」，where は「身体のどこに問題があるのか」，how は「どのような痛みや不快感があるのか」，などの質問に応用できます。

when：When does the movie start?「その映画はいつ始まりますか？」
where：Where do you live?「どこに住んでいますか？」
how：How do you go to the office?「どのように通勤していますか？」
why：Why are you angry?「なぜ怒っているのですか？」

Exercise　次の日本語を英語に直しましょう。

1. いつ痛みが始まりましたか？

2. どこに痛みを感じますか？

• Unit 8 • How would you describe the pain?

D Patient Communication

🎵 17

❶ 音声をよく聞き，空欄に正しい英単語を入れましょう。

Healthcare Worker: Good morning. How are you ¹(　　　　)?

Patient: Good morning. Well, not too bad, but I couldn't sleep well last night. My knee hurt last night.

Healthcare Worker: OK. Then, how would you ²(　　　　) your pain? Is it a ³(　　　　) pain, or a ⁴(　　　　) pain?

Patient: Well, it's hard to describe it. But I think it's a ⁴(　　　　) pain.

Healthcare Worker: Then, how would you ⁵(　　　　) your pain on a scale of 10*?

Patient: It's about 6.

Healthcare Worker: OK. Don't worry. After surgery, it happens a lot.

> **notes**
>
> **surgery** 手術
> **a scale of 10** 臨床では図のようなペインスケール（pain scale）を使って，患者さんに痛みを10段階（0が最も痛みが少なく，10が最も痛みが強い）で自己評価してもらうことがあります。

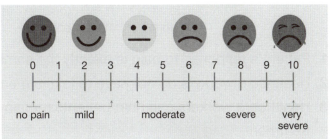

❷ 以下のステップに沿って，患者さんとの英語コミュニケーションの練習をしましょう。

Step 1. 音声に続いて会話練習（リピーティング）をしましょう。

Step 2. 先ほどのダイアローグに沿って，ペアで英語コミュニケーションの練習をしましょう。

39

E Reading Comprehension

❶ 英文を読んで，設問の内容が正しい場合は T，誤っている場合は F を選びましょう。

Pain Management

Most patients experience pain, but they respond differently* to it. Some patients are sensitive* to pain. Others are not. Medical workers must carefully observe their patients. These are the basic checkpoints:

A. What is the patient's pain level?
B. How does the patient describe their pain?
C. How does pain level increase or decrease over time?
D. Where is the pain located*, and how does that location* change?
E. Do painkillers* work*?

It is important for healthcare workers to write down these points and report them to other team members. By doing that, the patient is appropriately treated and remains comfortable during the treatment*.

 notes   respond differently / 異なった反応をする，sensitive / 敏感な，located / 〜にある，location / 場所，painkiller / 痛み止め work / 効く，treatment / 治療

1. Patient's response to pain is exactly the same. [T / F]
2. Healthcare workers do not have to take a memo about patient pain. [T / F]
3. Healthcare workers can help patients remain comfortable during the treatment. [T / F]

❷ 以下の Healthcare Worker の発言は上の英文の "basic check points" の A〜E のどれに当てはまるか考えましょう。

1. "How would you describe your pain? Is it an aching pain?" (   )
2. "How would you rate your pain?" (   )
3. "Where in your arm do you feel pain?" (   )

• Unit 8 • How would you describe the pain?

F Role Play

以下の２つのシーンで医療従事者が患者さんに痛みに関する質問をしています。例を参考にして，今まで学習した表現を使って英語コミュニケーションの練習をしましょう。

Scene 1

(Example) knee pain

Healthcare Workers: Hello, Mr. Yamada. How are you feeling?
Patient: I have pain in my knee.
Healthcare Workers: I see. How would you describe the pain?
Patient: It's an aching pain.
Healthcare Workers: Thank you. The doctor will come soon.

Scene 2

back pain

✎ memo
....
....
....
....
....
....
....

臨床現場からのメッセージ 8 　「痛みから分かること」

　リハビリの時は痛みが「鋭い」か「鈍い」か，という違いは大事です。なぜなら**鋭い痛みは急性**の場合が多く，**鈍い痛みの時は使い痛めなどの慢性痛**が多いからです。"dull pain" と "sharp pain" はぜひ覚えておきたい単語です。
　また，患者さんの飲んでいる薬から痛みの種類や程度を判断できます。これは外国人患者さんでも同じで，服用薬から多くの情報が分かります。外国人患者さんとのコミュニケーションには会話だけでなく，**薬の知識などからも多角的に情報を得る**ことが大切です。

UNIT 9
How much can you move your legs?

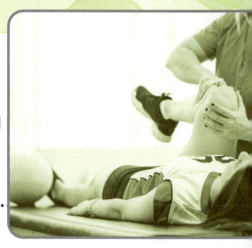

A Warm Up

各関節がどの程度動くかを「可動域」と言います。ではケガが原因で足の関節が一時的に曲がりづらくなった患者さんの可動域を回復されるには，どのような運動が良いでしょうか？ペアで考えましょう。

B Vocabulary

CD 18

以下の英単語の意味を選択肢の日本語を記号で選びましょう。

1. tight   [   ]   2. thigh   [   ]   3. nervous   [   ]
4. progress   [   ]   5. bend   [   ]   6. rehabilitation   [   ]

選択肢

a. ふともも   b. 進歩   c. 緊張した   d. 固い   e. 曲げる   f. リハビリ

Pronunciation Box

[p] と [b]

progress や bend に [p] と [b] の発音が含まれています。違いに注意して丁寧に発音しましょう。
[p]：無声音なので，唇を弾かせ，「プッ プッ」と空気を吐き出し発音します。
[b]：有声音なので，[p] の発音のまま喉を震わせて音を出します。

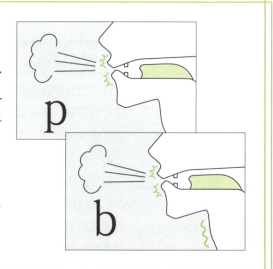

• Unit 9 • How much can you move your legs?

C Useful Expressions for Patient Communication

以下は患者さんとの英語コミュニケーションでよく使用される表現です。正しい意味を選択肢から選びましょう。

Healthcare Worker の表現

1. I'd like to see how much you can move your legs. [　]
2. Could you bring your right thigh toward your chest? [　]
3. Can you go any further? [　]
4. You're making good progress! [　]

Patient の表現

5. I'm a little nervous. [　]
6. It sounds painful. [　]
7. My muscles are tight. [　]
8. I can't bend any further. [　]

選択肢

a. 筋肉が張っています。
b. 脚をどれくらい動かせるか見てみたいと思います。
c. それは痛そうですね。
d. もう少しできますか？
e. 少し緊張しています。
f. 右太ももを胸の方に持ってきていただけますか？
g. これ以上曲げられません。
h. 順調に進んでいますよ！

Grammar Box　　　依頼

丁寧な依頼表現として「Would you + 動詞の原形」や「Could you + 動詞の原形」の形があり、「〜していただけますか？」という意味になります。

例：Would you help me?「手伝ってもらえますか？」
例：Could you take a deep breath?「深呼吸できますか？」

Exercise　次の日本語を英語に直しましょう。

1. 窓を開けてもらえますか？

2. 両手をあげられますか？

43

D Patient Communication

 19

❶ 音声をよく聞き，以下のスクリプトの空欄に正しい英単語を入れましょう。

Healthcare Worker: Hello. I'd like to see how much you can move your legs.

Patient: OK. But I'm a little ¹(   ). It ²(   ) painful.

Healthcare Worker: Please let me know if you have any pain. I'll move it slowly.

Patient: I see. Let's start.

Healthcare Worker: OK. Could you bring your left ³(   ) toward your chest?

Patient: Like this?

Healthcare Worker: Good! Can you ⁴(   ) any further?

Patient: Mmm. My muscles are tight, and I can't bend any further.

Healthcare Worker: Don't worry. You're making good ⁵(   )!

❷ 以下のステップに沿って，患者さんとの英語コミュニケーションの練習をしましょう。

Step 1. 音声に続いて会話練習（リピーティング）をしましょう。

Step 2. 先ほどのダイアローグに沿って，ペアで英語コミュニケーションの練習をしましょう。

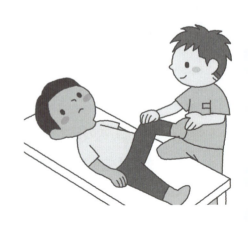

E Reading Comprehension

❶ 英文を読んで，設問の内容が正しい場合はT，誤っている場合はFを選びましょう。

Communication Techniques for Successful Rehabilitation

For successful rehabilitation, healthcare workers need to talk to the patients in a helpful way*. Here, we'll show some examples of good communication.

Encouragement and praise

In rehabilitation, encouragement* is important. But just saying "Good!" is not enough. Give more specific encouragement. For example, say "Your legs are moving very well!" or "Your balance when walking is good." Healthcare workers should also help patients feel hopeful*. You can say "Your balance when walking is good. You'll be able to go shopping very soon!"

Understand and share feelings

Many patients feel pain during rehabilitation. They want others to understand their feelings. If the patient says, "My leg hurts even when I'm lying down*," you can say, "Oh, does it hurt even when you're lying down? It must be hard to sleep well." In this way, you can share feelings with them.

notes　in a helpful way / 助けになるような方法で
　　　　　encouragement / 励まし，hopeful / 希望を持った，lie down / 横になる

1. Healthcare workers should use simple expressions for encouragement.　　[T / F]
2. Healthcare workers should not mention future improvement.　　[T / F]
3. Patients want to share their feelings with others.　　[T / F]

❷ 以下の Healthcare Worker の発言は上の英文の "Encouragement and praise" あるいは "Understand and share feelings" のどれに当てはまるか考えましょう。

1. "You've made incredible progress!"　　(　　　　　　　　)
2. "I know rehabilitation isn't easy. It's natural to feel frustrated sometimes."
　　　　　　　　　　　　　　　　　　　　　　　　(　　　　　　　　)
3. "You've improved so much since we started."　(　　　　　　　　)

F Role Play

以下の２つのシーンで医療従事者が患者さんの可動域の確認をしています。例を参考にして，今まで学習した表現を使って英語コミュニケーションの練習をしましょう。

Scene 1

(Example) bend one's knees

Healthcare Worker: Hello. I'd like to see how much you can move your knees. Could you lie on your back?

Patient: Like this?

Healthcare Worker: That's right. Then, can you bend your knees?

Patient: Mmm. Like this? I can't bend them any further.

Healthcare Worker: Don't worry. You're making good progress!

Scene 2

straighten one's knees

✎ memo

....
....
....
....
....
....
....

臨床現場からのメッセージ9 「リハビリ時のコミュニケーション」

リハビリの際は患者さんと**コミュニケーションをしっかりとりましょう**。まず相手をよく見て，反応を丁寧に観察することが大切です。可動域を確認する時は，患者さんの表情や顔色を見ながら，痛みの出る場所を確認していきます。必要に応じてアイコンタクトを取りながら声掛けをして，**患者さんに安心感を与える**ことも大事です。外国人患者さんへの声かけは"OK？"など，**簡単な表現から始める**とよいと思います。

UNIT 10
Let's start practicing getting into the wheelchair

A Warm Up

患者さんが安全に車いすに乗れるようにサポートするのも大切なリハビリです。では脚を骨折して歩けない患者さんをベッドから車いすに移乗させる時，どのような声かけが必要でしょうか？ペアで考えましょう。

B Vocabulary

CD 20

以下の英単語の意味を選択肢の日本語を記号で選びましょう。

1. wheelchair　[　]　2. injured　[　]　3. count　[　]
4. confused　[　]　5. get into〜　[　]　6. a lack of 〜　[　]

選択肢

a. 混乱して　b. けがをして　c. 車いす　d. 〜に乗る　e. 〜の不足　f. 数える

Pronunciation Box

[w] と [j]

wheelchair に [w] の発音が含まれています。[j] との違いに注意して丁寧に発音しましょう。
[w]：唇を丸くすぼめた状態で喉を震わせながら息を吐き出し，それと同時に唇の力を緩めます。
[j]：上あごの硬い部分に舌の先を近づけ，その状態で喉を震わせ「ヤ」と「イ」の間のような音を出します。

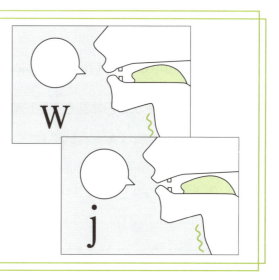

C Useful Expressions for Patient Communication

以下は患者さんとの英語コミュニケーションでよく使用される表現です。正しい意味を選択肢から選びましょう。

Healthcare Worker の表現

1. Let's start practicing getting into the wheelchair. [ ]
2. Put your arms over my neck. [ ]
3. After I say, "one, two, three", stand up. [ ]
4. We did a wonderful job! [ ]

Patient の表現

5. I'll try to do it slowly. [ ]
6. Like this? [ ]
7. Thank you for helping me! [ ]

選択肢

a. 車いすに乗る練習を始めましょう。
b. 私たちはよく頑張りました！
c. ゆっくりとやってみます。
d. 1・2・3と言った後に立ってください。
e. 手伝ってくださってありがとうございます。
f. 私の首に腕を回してください。
g. これでいいですか？

Grammar Box　　命令文

命令文は何かを**命令**したり，**指示**や**助言**をする時に使います。命令文は動詞の原形を文頭に置きます。

例：Sit at the edge of the bed, please.「ベッドの端に座ってください。」

Exercise 次の日本語を英語に直しましょう。

1. 口を開けて，「あー」と言ってください。

2. シャツを脱いでください。

• Unit 10 • Let's start practicing getting into the wheelchair

D Patient Communication

 21

❶ 音声をよく聞き，空欄に正しい英単語を入れましょう。

Healthcare Worker: Let's ¹(　　　　　) ²(　　　　　　) getting into the wheelchair.

Patient: OK. I'm a little nervous, but I'll try to do it slowly.

Healthcare Worker: Good! Then put your ³(　　　　　　) over my neck.

Patient: Like this?

Healthcare Worker: Yes. After I say, "one, two, three", stand up, and turn your hips toward the wheelchair slowly.

Patient: OK. I'll try to do it ⁴(　　　　　).

Healthcare Worker: One…, two…, three!

Patient: Whew!

Healthcare Worker: Great! We did a wonderful job!

Patient: Thank you for ⁵(　　　　) me!

❷ 以下のステップに沿って，患者さんとの英語コミュニケーションの練習をしましょう。

Step 1. 音声に続いて会話練習（リピーティング）をしましょう。

Step 2. 先ほどのダイアローグに沿って，ペアで英語コミュニケーションの練習をしましょう。

E Reading Comprehension

❶ 英文を読んで，設問の内容が正しい場合は T，誤っている場合は F を選びましょう。

Helping Patients Get into a Wheelchair

When you help patients get into a wheelchair, you must be careful. Communication is important because patients often get injured because of a lack of communication. If the patient is not ready, they may become confused and may fall down*. Therefore, you must explain what you are going to do before you start. Then, count "one, two, three" before you start. This can help the patient get ready. Also, you should help relax the patient. If a patient can't stand up on their own, they may feel anxious. Talk to them and help them relax.

notes　fall down / 転倒する

1. If the patient is not ready to get into a wheelchair, he or she may get injured. [T / F]
2. It is unnecessary to explain the procedure before helping a patient get into a wheelchair. [T / F]
3. Conversation is important to help relax patients. [T / F]

❷ 以下の Healthcare Worker の発言は上の英文の "help patient get ready" あるいは "relax the patient" のどれに当てはまるか考えましょう。

1. "After I say, "one, two, three", stand up."
(　　　　　　　　　　　　　　　)

2. "You can try to do it slowly."
(　　　　　　　　　　　　　　　)

• Unit 10 • Let's start practicing getting into the wheelchair

F Role Play

以下は車いすへの移乗を介助する動作です。Healthcare Worker と Patient に分かれて，実際に英語でコミュニケーションをしながら，移乗介助をしましょう。

Scene 1	Scene 2	Scene 3

✎ memo

臨床現場からのメッセージ 10　「基本フレーズ表を車いすに付けておくと便利」

　私が勤務している病院の外国人患者さんは中国人，韓国人，ギリシャ人が多いです。アメリカ人などの学校の英語の先生もいます。外国人患者さんは日本在住の方が多いですが，本人は片言の日本語しか話せず，子供が日本語を話せるケースが多いです。英語ならまだしも，ギリシャ語などは全然わかりませんので，ご家族の方に「今からリハビリを始めます」や「立てますか」などの**基本フレーズをカタカナで書いてもらい，それを車いすに付けておくと**，必要なときにすぐに使えて便利です。

51

Let's make the walks longer

A Warm Up

リハビリには色々な道具や機器が使用されます。専門的な機器はもちろん，日常生活で見かけるものもあります。では，具体的にどのような道具や機器があるでしょうか？ペアで考えましょう。

B Vocabulary

CD 22

以下の英単語の意味を選択肢の日本語を記号で選びましょう。

1. handrail　　[　]　　2. exercise　　[　]　　3. method　　[　]
4. little by little　[　]　　5. go well　　[　]　　6. hold onto ～　[　]

選択肢

a. 少しずつ　　b. うまくいく　　c. 方法　　d. 手すり　　e. 運動　　f. ～につかまる

Pronunciation Box

[t] と [d]

handrail や method に [d] の発音が含まれています。[t] との違いに注意して丁寧に発音しましょう。
[t]：無声音なので，少し口を開き，前歯の間を狭くしたまま，上の前歯の生え際に舌先をつけ，舌を弾かせながら後ろに引いて発音します。
[d]：有声音なので，[t] の発音のまま喉を震わせて音を出します。

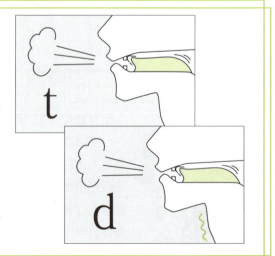

• Unit 11 • Let's make the walks longer

C Useful Expressions for Patient Communication

以下は患者さんとの英語コミュニケーションでよく使用される表現です。正しい意味を選択肢から選びましょう。

Healthcare Worker の表現

1. Is the rehabilitation going well? [ ]
2. I'd like to see how you walk. [ ]
3. Let's make the walks longer little by little. [ ]

Patient の表現

4. I'm getting better little by little. [ ]
5. Can I use the handrail for support? [ ]
6. I was able to walk three steps. [ ]

選択肢

a. 少しずつ良くなっています。　b. どのように歩くか見せてください。
c. 3歩歩くことができました。　d. リハビリは順調に進んでいますか？
e. 少しずつ歩く距離を伸ばしましょう。
f. 手すりを支えに使ってもいいですか？

Grammar Box　　　　　比較

2つの物事や状態を比較するには，語尾に "-er" を使う場合と more「もっと」を用いる場合があります。

1. -er の場合：
例：My car is faster than yours.「私の車はあなたの車よりも速いです。」
2. more〜の場合：
例：This book is more interesting than that one.
　「この本はあの本よりも面白いです。」
例：She sings more beautifully than others.
　「彼女はほかの人よりも美しく歌います。」

Exercise　次の日本語を英語に直しましょう。

1. 今日は昨日よりも暖かいです。

　..

2. 昨日よりも痛みを感じます。

　..

53

D Patient Communication

 23

❶ 音声をよく聞き，以下のスクリプトの空欄に正しい英単語を入れましょう。

Healthcare Worker: Hello, how are you today? Is the rehabilitation ¹(   ) ²(   )?

Patient: Hello. Yes, I think I'm getting better little by little.

Healthcare Worker: Good. Today, I'd like to see how you walk.

Patient: Can I ³(   ) the ⁴(   ) for support?

Healthcare Worker: Of course, you can. Let's do it slowly.

Patient: OK. I'll do my best. … Whew*, I was ⁵(   ) to walk three steps.

Healthcare Worker: That's great progress! Let's make the walks longer little by little.

notes

whew （喜びや安堵，驚きなどを表して）ふぅ

❷ 以下のステップに沿って，患者さんとの英語コミュニケーションの練習をしましょう。

Step 1. 音声に続いて会話練習（リピーティング）をしましょう。

Step 2. 先ほどのダイアローグに沿って，ペアで英語コミュニケーションの練習をしましょう。

E Reading Comprehension

❶ 英文を読んで，設問の内容が正しい場合は T，誤っている場合は F を選びましょう。

Two Types of Rehabilitation Exercises

Physical therapists* use different methods for rehabilitation. Exercise is one of these methods. There are two types of exercises.

*Passive exercise**

Passive exercise is done by a therapist. Patients lie down on a bed. A physical therapist gently lifts and moves the patient's leg. This exercise can stretch their muscles.

*Active exercise**

Active exercise is done by the patients. For example, patients practice walking by holding onto handrails. Active exercise can be done both in the hospital and at home. A therapist guides patients and helps their recovery.

Both exercises play important roles in the rehabilitation process.

notes   physical therapist / 作業療法士, passive exercise / 他動運動
active exercise / 自動運動

1. Passive exercise is performed by patients themselves.　　[T / F]
2. Active exercise can only be done in the hospital, not at home.　　[T / F]
3. Active exercise is more effective than passive exercise.　　[T / F]

❷ 以下のイラストは上の英文の "Passive exercise" あるいは "Active exercise" のどれに当てはまるか考えましょう。

1.　　　　　　　　2.　　　　　　　　3.

(　　　　　) (　　　　　　　　) (　　　　　　　　　　　)

F Role Play

以下の２つのシーンでそれぞれの患者さんがリハビリを行っています。例を参考にして，今まで学習した表現を使って英語コミュニケーションの練習をしましょう。

Scene 1

(Example) walk

Healthcare Worker: Today, I'd like to see how you walk.
Patient: OK. I'll do my best.
Healthcare Worker: You can use the handrail for support.
Patient: OK. I'll do it slowly. … Whew, I was able to walk five steps.
Healthcare Worker: That's great progress! Let's make the walks longer little by little.

Scene 2

go up the stairs

✎ *memo*

....
....
....
....
....
....

臨床現場からのメッセージ 11 ｜「励まし方にもコツがある」

励ますのは難しいです。安直な言葉がけは患者さんに響きませんし，逆に反発されることもあります。私が担当した患者さんで手のリハビリをしている方なのですが，その方は書道の先生をしていました。その方を励ますつもりで，「また書道ができるようにがんばりましょう」と言ってしまうのは NG です。「そんなの無理に決まってる！」や「もうあんな風には書けない！」と反発されてしまうからです。書道にはあえて触れずに，お箸を持つなど，日常的な動作で**小さな目標から励ましていく**のがいいでしょう。私の場合は患者さんの気持ちが上向いて本人から書道の話をするのを待ち，その時に**長期的な目標**として書道を提案します。

UNIT 12

You're from Australia, aren't you?

A Warm Up

患者さんとの何気ない会話から信頼関係を築くことができます。患者さんとの雑談には，どのような話題が良いでしょうか？ペアで考えましょう。

B Vocabulary

CD 24

以下の英単語の意味を選択肢の日本語を記号で選びましょう。

1. opposite   [   ]   2. situation   [   ]   3. conversation   [   ]
4. hurt   [   ]   5. affect   [   ]   6. chat with〜   [   ]

選択肢

a. 〜と世間話をする   b. 反対の   c. 会話   d. 影響する   e. 痛む   f. 状況

Pronunciation Box

[ɑ] と [ɑː]

opposite や conversation に [ɑ] の発音が含まれています。[ɑː] との違いに注意して丁寧に発音しましょう。
[ɑ]：口は日本語の「オ」の形にして「ア」と発音します。舌は上あごからなるべく遠くに置き，口のなかのスペースを広くして発音します。
[ɑː]：[ɑ] と同じ方法で，音を伸ばして発音します。

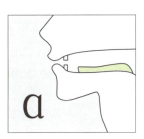

C Useful Expressions for Patient Communication

以下は患者さんとの英語コミュニケーションでよく使用される表現です。正しい意味を選択肢から選びましょう。

Healthcare Worker の表現

1. It's cold outside. [ ]
2. You're from Australia, aren't you? [ ]
3. The seasons in Australia and Japan are opposite, aren't they? [ ]
4. If you find your room a little cold, please let us know. [ ]

Patient の表現

5. It's warm inside the hospital. [ ]
6. I was surprised by the cold. [ ]

選択肢

a. 病院の中は暖かいです。
b. 外は寒いですよ。
c. もしお部屋が少し寒いと感じれば，教えてください。
d. あなたはオーストラリア出身ですよね？
e. オーストラリアと日本は季節が反対ですよね？
f. 寒さに驚きました。

Grammar Box　　付加疑問文

「〜ですよね？」と相手に確認や同意を求める表現を付加疑問文と呼びます。

1. 肯定文の場合：「〜isn't / aren't ＋主語？」あるいは「〜don't / doesn't ＋主語？」
例：She is from Australia, isn't she?「彼女はオーストラリア出身ですよね？」
例：You like coffee, don't you?「コーヒーは好きですよね？」

2. 否定文の場合：「〜is / are ＋主語？」あるいは「〜do / does ＋主語？」
例：She isn't from Canada, is she?「彼女はカナダ出身ではないですよね？」
例：You don't like coffee, do you?「コーヒーは好きではないですよね？」

Exercise 次の日本語を英語に直しましょう。

1. 彼は宿題を終えましたよね？

   ....

2. まだランチを食べてないですよね？

   ....

• Unit 12 • You're from Australia, aren't you?

D Patient Communication

 25

❶ 音声をよく聞き，以下のスクリプトの空欄に正しい英単語を入れましょう。

Healthcare Worker: Hello. It's cold outside.

Patient: Oh, really? It's ¹(   ) inside the hospital, so I don't really feel it.

Healthcare Worker: You're from Australia, aren't you?

Patient: Yes, I'm from Sydney.

Healthcare Worker: The seasons in Australia and Japan are ²(   ), aren't they?

Patient: It's summer in Australia right now. So I was surprised by the cold here.

Healthcare Worker: If you find your room a ³(   ) ⁴(   ), please let us ⁵(   ).

Patient: Thank you.

❷ 以下のステップに沿って，患者さんとの英語コミュニケーションの練習をしましょう。

Step 1. 音声に続いて会話練習（リピーティング）をしましょう。

Step 2. 先ほどのダイアローグに沿って，ペアで英語コミュニケーションの練習をしましょう。

59

E Reading Comprehension

❶ 英文を読んで，設問の内容が正しい場合は T，誤っている場合は F を選びましょう。

Communication Skills for New Healthcare Workers

Chatting with patients is sometimes difficult for new healthcare workers. They cannot find topics or continue a conversation because they have only talked to their friends. But in hospitals, they have to talk to older people or foreign people. New healthcare workers often say, "It's raining today." Weather is a good topic, but the conversation doesn't continue. In this situation, you can say "It's raining today. Does your injury hurt more?". From this question, you can ask the patient if the weather affects their pain. Or "It's raining today. What do you usually do on rainy days?" is also good. From this question, you can learn about patients' lifestyle habits.

1. New healthcare workers may find it challenging to chat with patients.　　[T / F]
2. New healthcare workers are not familiar with talking to old people. [T / F]
3. Healthcare workers should not talk about weather with their patients.　　[T / F]

❷ 本文の内容を踏まえて，空欄に入る最も適切な表現を選択肢から選びましょう。

Healthcare Worker: I noticed you have a picture of a beautiful garden by your bed. Do you enjoy gardening?

Patient: Yes, I do. Gardening is my hobby. I find it very relaxing.

Healthcare Worker: (　　)

選択肢

a. That's wonderful! I like gardening too.
b. It's good to hear that.　　　　　　　　　　　　　　　　　(　　)
c. Then, we could walk to the hospital garden. It would make you feel better.

• Unit 12 • You're from Australia, aren't you?

F Role Play

以下の２つのシーンで医療従事者と患者さんが天気に関する会話をしています。例を参考にして，今まで学習した表現を使って英語コミュニケーションの練習をしましょう。

Scene 1
(Example) snowing

Healthcare Worker: Hello. It's snowing outside.

Patient: Yes, it is. But It's warm inside the hospital, isn't it?

Healthcare Worker: Yes, it is. Does your injury hurt more in this weather?

Patient: I'm fine, thank you.

Healthcare Worker: If you find your room a little cold, please let us know.

Patient: Thank you.

Scene 2
hot

✏️ memo
....
....
....
....

臨床現場からのメッセージ 12 　「信頼関係を築くには」

　医療従事者と患者さんとの間では，どうしても壁ができやすいです。患者さんが外国人の場合，言葉や文化の違いもあります。そのため，患者さんとの**何気ない会話から距離を縮める**ことが大切です。例えば，自分の専門領域や治療経験などを患者さんに話すと安心感を与えられます。また患者さんが医師と話す時間は限られているので，看護師やリハビリ技師に相談がきます。「最近アレルギーで鼻炎がひどいのよ」など現在の疾患に関係ない健康相談も多いです。その場合は単に「○○科に相談しますか？」と言うだけでなく，「食事や睡眠などで免疫を高められますよ」など，もう少し**具体的なアドバイス**ができるといいでしょう。患者さんにとって看護師やリハスタッフは**親しみやすい先生とみられる**こともあります。日々のやり取りを通して信頼関係を築きましょう。

61

UNIT 13

Are you Ms. Brown?

A Warm Up

医療従事者にとって，患者さんだけでなくご家族の方とのコミュニケーションも重要です。ご家族の方と話す時，どのような点に気をつければよいでしょうか。ペアで考えましょう。

B Vocabulary

CD 26

以下の英単語の意味を選択肢の日本語を記号で選びましょう。

1. worried　　[　]　　2. effective　　[　]　　3. interrupt　　[　]
4. active　　[　]　　5. sound like〜　[　]　　6. cope with〜　[　]

選択肢

a. 効果的な　　b. 積極的な　　c. 〜そうだ　　d. 〜に対処する　　e. 心配した　　f. 邪魔する

Pronunciation Box

[ʌ] と [æ]

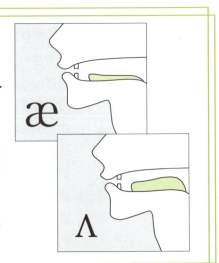

interrupt や active に [ʌ] と [æ] の発音が含まれています。違いに注意して丁寧に発音しましょう。

[æ]：日本語の「ア」と「エ」の間のような音で，口を横に少し引き，舌は下あごに張り付くようにして口の中のスペースは広めにしたままで発音します。

[ʌ]：日本語の「ア」に近い音ですが，日本語のように口を大きく開けません。口の開きを狭めて舌は口の下の方に置いて，後ろに少し引いて発音します。

C Useful Expressions for Patient Communication

以下は患者さんとの英語コミュニケーションでよく使用される表現です。正しい意味を選択肢から選びましょう。

Healthcare Worker の表現

1. It's natural to feel anxious about something new. [ ]
2. We're here to support you. [ ]
3. Reading is a great way to relax. [ ]

Patient の表現

4. This is our first time in a hospital in Japan. [ ]
5. We are a little worried. [ ]
6. That's good to know. [ ]

選択肢

a. 読書はリラックスするのに良い方法です。
b. 日本で入院するのは初めてです。
c. 私たちは少し心配しています。
d. 新しいことに不安を感じるのは自然なことです。
e. それを知れてよかったです。
f. 私たちはあなたをサポートするためにここにいます。

Grammar Box　　　　仮主語

「**It is** + 形容詞 + **to** + 動詞の原形」の形で「~するのは…である」という意味になります。また「**for** + 人」を間に入れて「**It is** + 形容詞 + **for** + 人 + **to** + 動詞の原形」の形で、「○○が~するのは…である」という意味になります。

例：It is important to study for exams.
　　「試験のために勉強することは重要です。」
例：It is important for students to study for exams.
　　「学生が試験のために勉強することは重要です。」

Exercise 次の日本語を英語に直しましょう。

1. 十分な睡眠をとることは重要です。

2. 一部の患者（some patients）にとっては生活習慣を変えることは難しいです。

D Patient Communication

❶ 音声をよく聞き，以下のスクリプトの空欄に正しい英単語を入れましょう。

Healthcare Worker: Hello. Are you Ms. Brown?

Ms. Brown: Yes, I am. This is our first time in a ¹(　　　　) in Japan. We're a little worried.

Healthcare Worker: I see. It's natural to ²(　　　　) ³(　　　　) about something new, but we're here to ⁴(　　　　) you.

Ms. Brown: Thank you. He recently started reading as a hobby.

Healthcare Worker: That's wonderful! Reading is a great way to ⁵(　　　　). What kind of books does he enjoy?

Ms. Brown: He likes mystery novels.

Healthcare Worker: We have a library here. You'll find some English books.

Ms. Brown: That's good to know. Thank you very much.

❷ 以下のステップに沿って，患者さんとの英語コミュニケーションの練習をしましょう。

Step 1. 音声に続いて会話練習（リピーティング）をしましょう。

Step 2. 先ほどのダイアローグに沿って，ペアで英語コミュニケーションの練習をしましょう。

• Unit 13 • Are you Ms. Brown?

E Reading Comprehension

❶ 英文を読んで，設問の内容が正しい場合は T，誤っている場合は F を選びましょう。

Four Important Points for Active Listening.

Healthcare workers do not often meet with patients' families. So, the key to communicating with them is "active listening." Active listening is good for effective communication. What is it? Here are four important points for active listening:

Don't disagree
When families talk to you, don't disagree. Try to understand their point of view.

Show your understanding
Try to understand their feelings. If they're sad, you don't have to make them happy right away. You can just say, "It sounds like you're feeling sad."

Listen until they finish
When families are talking, don't interrupt. This is especially important when you talk to foreign patients, because they cannot speak Japanese well.

Non-verbal communication
Communication is done not just by words. Your face, gestures, and body language are also important. Don't forget to smile.

Families sometimes cannot cope with the illness and become confused. For these people, active listening is effective.

1. Active listening is a good conversation technique to talk with patients' families. 　　　　　　　　　　　　　　　　　　　　　　　[T / F]

2. It is recommended to disagree with families to show a different perspective. 　　　　　　　　　　　　　　　　　　　　　　　　　　　[T / F]

3. Interrupting families while they are talking is acceptable in certain situations. 　　　　　　　　　　　　　　　　　　　　　　　　　　　[T / F]

❷ active listening になるように，空欄に入る最も適切な表現を選択肢から選びましょう。

　　　　　　Patient: My pain is getting worse, and I cannot sleep well.
Healthcare Worker: (　　　)

選択肢

a. Please relax. Did you take your medicine as prescribed?

b. Just follow the doctor's instructions. You will start to feel better soon.　　(　　　)

c. It's natural to feel anxious. It must be really hard for you.

65

F Role Play

以下の2つのシーンでそれぞれの患者さんが最近始めた趣味について話をしています。例を参考にして，今まで学習した表現を使って英語コミュニケーションの練習をしましょう。

Scene 1

(Example) reading

Healthcare Worker: Hello. Are you Ms. White?

Ms. White: Yes, I am. We are a little anxious because this is our first time in a hospital in Japan.

Healthcare Worker: It's natural to feel that way. Don't worry. We're here to support you.

Ms. White: Thank you. He recently started reading as a hobby.

Healthcare Worker: That's wonderful! Reading is a great way to relax.

Scene 2

walking

✏️ memo

....
....
....

臨床現場からのメッセージ 13 ｜「誰から褒められるかも大切」

リハビリをしている患者さんにとって，リハビリの成果をほめてもらえることは，とても励みになります。実は**誰から褒められるか**，ということも大切です。リハビリスタッフから「できるようになりましたね」と言われるよりも，それ以外の看護師や医師から「〇〇さんはリハビリをすごく頑張っていると聞きましたよ。順調に進んでいますよ」や「この間〇〇さんがリハビリをしている所を見たけど，一生懸命されていますね」などと言われると，**患者さんの気持ちがすごく上向きます**。患者さんにとってリハビリスタッフに褒めてもらうのは，ある意味で当たり前みたいになっているので，それ以外の医療スタッフからの声掛けは励みになるようです。外国人患者さんの場合は難しいかもしれませんので，ご**家族の協力を得る**と良いかもしれません。

Rehabilitation can be challenging

A Warm Up

患者さんが治療やリハビリに前向きに取り組めるよう励ますことは非常に重要です。しかし，落ち込んでいる患者さんを励ますことは簡単ではありません。どのような点に注意して声かけをすればよいでしょうか？ペアで考えましょう。

B Vocabulary

🎵 28

以下の英単語の意味を選択肢の日本語を記号で選びましょう。

1. down   [   ]   2. challenging   [   ]   3. encouraging   [   ]
4. distance   [   ]   5. impolite   [   ]   6. do one's best [   ]

選択肢

a. 励みになる   b. 大変な   c. ベストを尽くす   d. 無礼な   e. 落ち込んだ   f. 距離

Pronunciation Box

[tʃ] と [dʒ]

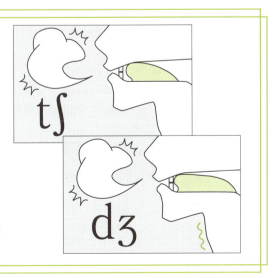

challenging や encouraging に [tʃ] と [dʒ] の発音が含まれています。

[tʃ]：無声音なので，前歯を合わせて舌先より少し手前の部分を上の前歯の歯茎あたりにつけ，舌を離した瞬間に息を通して発音します。

[dʒ]：有声音なので，[tʃ] の発音のまま喉を震わせて音を出します。

C Useful Expressions for Patient Communication

以下は患者さんとの英語コミュニケーションでよく使用される表現です。正しい意味を選択肢から選びましょう。

Healthcare Worker の表現

1. How is your rehabilitation going? [　]
2. Rehabilitation can be challenging. [　]
3. What seems to be the problem? [　]
4. Let's try to walk longer distances little by little. [　]

Patient の表現

5. I'm feeling a little down about it. [　]
6. I can't move my legs the way I want to. [　]
7. It's encouraging to hear that. [　]

選択肢

a. それについて少し落ち込んでいます。
b. リハビリは大変かもしれません。
c. 少しずつ長い距離を歩いてみましょう。
d. それを聞いて励みになります。　e. どうされましたか？
f. 思うように足を動かせません。　g. リハビリの調子はどうですか？

Grammar Box　　　助動詞

助動詞は「助動詞＋動詞の原形」の形で使います。代表的な助動詞は以下の通りです。

1. can「～できる」「～かもしれない」
   例：I can speak Spanish fluently.「私はスペイン語を流暢に話せます。」
2. should「～すべきである」
   例：Students should focus on their studies.「生徒たちは勉強に集中すべきです。」
3. must「～しなければならない」
   例：I must finish this report.「私はこのレポートを終えなければなりません。」
4. may「かもしれない」
   例：She may join us for dinner.「彼女は夕食に参加するかもしれません。」

Exercise　次の日本語を英語に直しましょう。

1. 医療従事者は患者に親切でなければなりません。

2. 健康のためにお酒を飲むのをやめるべきです。

D Patient Communication

 29

❶ 音声をよく聞き，以下のスクリプトの空欄に正しい英単語を入れましょう。

Healthcare Worker: Hello, how are you today? How is your rehabilitation going?

Patient: Well, it's not going well. I'm feeling a little down about it.

Healthcare Worker: I see. Rehabilitation can be ¹(   ). What seems to be the ²(   )?

Patient: I can't move my ³(   ) the way I want to… I'm very stressed.

Healthcare Worker: It's OK. Progress might take some time. Let's try to walk longer ⁴(   ) little by little.

Patient: Thank you. It's ⁵(   ) to hear that. I'm feeling better now.

❷ 以下のステップに沿って，患者さんとの英語コミュニケーションの練習をしましょう。

Step 1. 音声に続いて会話練習（リピーティング）をしましょう。

Step 2. 先ほどのダイアローグに沿って，ペアで英語コミュニケーションの練習をしましょう。

E Reading Comprehension

❶ 英文を読んで，設問の内容が正しい場合は T，誤っている場合は F を選びましょう。

Phrases to Avoid

When you talk to patients, there are some phrases you should not use.

"Do your best."
Saying "Do your best." sometimes puts pressure on patients. It does not have any negative meanings, but you should understand the patient's situation before you use it. It is good to say, "Let's do our best together."

"I'm busy."
Even if you are busy, you should not say, "I'm busy now. Please wait." Some patients may think it is impolite. Others may feel anxious. In this case, you should say, "Please wait here. I'll call another staff member. He'll be here in a few minutes."

Even small changes in our words can make a big difference to patients. You should carefully choose your words.

1. "Do your best" always has a negative impact on patients. [T / F]
2. "Let's do our best together" is considered better than "Do your best." [T / F]
3. Small changes in words greatly affect how patients feel. [T / F]

❷ 本文の内容を踏まえて，空欄に入る最も適切な表現を選択肢から選びましょう。

　　　　　Patient: I'm a little nervous during the rehabilitation. I don't think my arms are getting better.
Healthcare Worker: (　　)

選択肢

a. Do your best! You can do it!　　b. Why don't you do your best?　　(　　)
c. Let's try setting some small goals. Let's do our best together to achieve them!

• Unit 14 • Rehabilitation can be challenging

F Role Play

以下の2つのシーンで落ち込む患者さんを医療従事者が励ましています。例を参考にして，今まで学習した表現を使って英語コミュニケーションの練習をしましょう。

Scene 1

(Example) walk

Healthcare Worker: What seems to be the problem?

Patient: Rehabilitation is not going well. I can't move my legs the way I want to...

Healthcare Worker: I see. Progress might take some time. Let's try to walk longer distances little by little.

Patient: Thank you. It's encouraging to hear that.

Scene 2

bend arms

memo

....
....
....
....
....

臨床現場からのメッセージ 14 「「頑張る」は，確かに難しい」

患者さんを励ます時は，やはり言葉を選びます。特に「頑張ってください」という言葉は難しいです。「私もお手伝いするので，一緒にがんばりましょう」など，**患者さんだけに負担を背負わせないような言葉**づかいを心がけています。「あなたのがんばり次第です」などもNGワードです。

ただ患者さんの中には明らかに余裕があって，もっとリハビリを進めなければいけないケースもあります。その時は「〇〇さん，もっと頑張りましょう」と言いながら，具体的な目標を出すようにしています。ケースバイケースで，**その人の性格や病状などを総合的に見る必要が**あります。

71

By working together, we can ease your concerns

A Warm Up

症状が改善しない場合や，思い通りにリハビリが進まない場合などで，患者さんが落ち込んだり，ふさぎ込むことがあります。その際は，どのような対応が良いでしょうか？ペアで考えましょう。

B Vocabulary

CD 30

以下の英単語の意味を選択肢の日本語を記号で選びましょう。

1. share　　　[　]
2. normal　　[　]
3. expect　　[　]
4. minimize　[　]
5. discomfort [　]
6. ease　　　[　]

選択肢

a. 伝える・共有する　b. 予想する　c. 普通な　d. 不快感　e. やわらげる　f. 最小限にする

Pronunciation Box

[m], [n], [ŋ]

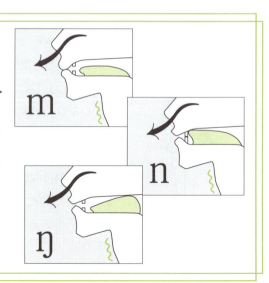

normal, minimize や discomfort に [m] や [n] の発音が含まれています。[ŋ] との違いに注意して丁寧に発音しましょう。
[m]：口を閉じた状態で日本語の「ン」に近い音を鼻から息を出しながら発音します。
[n]：唇を少しだけあけて，舌先を上の前歯の歯茎につけます。その状態で鼻から息を出しながら喉を震わせて音を出します。
[ŋ]：舌の根本のほうが上あごとくっついた状態で，鼻から息を出しながら上あごについていた舌を離して「グ」に近い音を出します。

• Unit 15 • By working together, we can ease your concerns

C Useful Expressions for Patient Communication

以下は患者さんとの英語コミュニケーションでよく使用される表現です。正しい意味を選択肢から選びましょう。

Healthcare Worker の表現

1. Please feel free to share anything. [　]
2. It's normal to feel that way. [　]
3. We will do our best to minimize your discomfort. [　]
4. By working together, we can ease your concerns. [　]

Patient の表現

5. I'm a bit anxious. [　]
6. How much pain can I expect? [　]
7. I'm feeling a little more positive now. [　]

選択肢

a. 何でも遠慮なく話してください。
b. そのように感じるのは普通ですよ。
c. 不快感を最小限にできるように最善を尽くします。
d. 少し心配しています。
e. 今は少し前向きな気持ちです。
f. どれくらいの痛みを予想すればよいですか？
g. 協力しあうことで，不安を和らげることができます。

Grammar Box　　不定詞・目的用法

不定詞は「**to＋動詞の原形**」の形で使用します。複数の用法がありますが，「～するために」（目的）の意味になる副詞用法がよく使用されます。

例：He exercises every day to stay healthy.
　　「彼は健康を保つために毎日運動します。」

Exercise　次の日本語を英語に直しましょう。

1. 私は海外旅行をするために英語を勉強しています。

   ....

2. 彼は薬をもらうために薬局（pharmacy）に行きました。

   ....

73

D Patient Communication

❶ 音声をよく聞き，以下のスクリプトの空欄に正しい英単語を入れましょう。

Healthcare Worker: Hello, how are you today? I heard you're anxious before the surgery. Please feel free to ¹(   ) anything.

Patient: Hello. Actually, I'm a bit anxious.

Healthcare Worker: I understand. It's normal to feel that way.

Patient: How much pain can I ²(   )?

Healthcare Worker: It is different from person to person, but we'll do our best to ³(   ) your ⁴(   ).

Patient: Thank you. But, I'm still anxious.

Healthcare Worker: I understand your anxiety. By working together, we can ease your ⁵(   ).

Patient: Thank you very much. I'm feeling a little more positive now.

❷ 以下のステップに沿って，患者さんとの英語コミュニケーションの練習をしましょう。

Step 1. 音声に続いて会話練習（リピーティング）をしましょう。

Step 2. 先ほどのダイアローグに沿って，ペアで英語コミュニケーションの練習をしましょう。

• Unit 15 • By working together, we can ease your concerns

E Reading Comprehension

❶ 英文を読んで，設問の内容が正しい場合は T，誤っている場合は F を選びましょう。

How to Care for Patients Who Feel Sad

For patients who feel sad, it's important for healthcare workers to observe and help.

Observation*
People who feel really sad might not want to talk much. In this case, don't force them to cheer up*. Healthcare workers should be kind, but not push them to be happy.

Offering help
However, if the observation period lasts* for a long time, the patient may lose the chance to open their minds. In this situation, healthcare workers can say, "If you have anything on your mind, please feel free to share." But you should not expect a quick answer. Patients may need time.

It is important for healthcare workers to determine the right timing for observation and offering help.

notes   observation / 観察，cheer up / 元気になる，last / 続く

1. Healthcare workers should make patients happy if the patients are sad.

[T / F]

2. Patients may lose the opportunity to open up if the observation period is too long.　　　　　　　　　　　　　　　　　　　　　　　[T / F]

3. Finding the right timing for observation and offering help is important.

[T / F]

❷ 本文の内容を踏まえて，空欄に入る最も適切な表現を選択肢から選びましょう。

Patient: I don't have much energy these days. I'm not really in the mood to talk.

Healthcare Worker: (　　　)

選択肢

a. I understand, and that's perfectly fine. If there's anything you feel like sharing, please talk to me anytime.　　　　　　　　　　　　　　　　　　(　　　)

b. I see. But you need to try to be more positive. Let's talk about what makes you sad.

c. Well, you can't just sit here and be sad. You need to actively participate in your rehabilitation.

75

F Role Play

以下の２つのシーンでそれぞれの患者さんがリハビリに対して不安を感じています。例を参考にして，今まで学習した表現を使って英語コミュニケーションの練習をしましょう。

Scene 1

(Example)
leg rehabilitation

Healthcare Worker: Hello, how are you today? Please feel free to share anything.

Patient: Hello. Actually, I'm a bit anxious about my leg rehabilitation.

Healthcare Worker: We'll do our best to minimize your discomfort. By working together, we can ease your concerns.

Patient: Thank you. I'm feeling a little more positive now.

Scene 2

arm rehabilitation

✎ memo

....
....
....
....

臨床現場からのメッセージ 15 「幅広い知識が必要」

　臨床現場では幅広い知識が必要になります。例えば，採血は主に看護師の業務ですが，実は**リハビリ担当の技師でも採血データの読み取りは必要なスキル**です。私の勤務している病院では，医師・看護師・リハビリ技師でカンファレンスを行います。その時に医師が採血結果のデータを配布し，データを読み取れる前提で治療計画やリハビリ計画を立てます。また在宅でのリハビリ訪問の際にも患者さんの状態を把握するデータとして，血液検査のデータを医師から渡されます。意外とよくあるのは，患者さんから血液検査の結果を見せられて，「この間の検査の結果をどう思う？」などと健康相談をされるケースです。病院では技師であっても患者さんから「先生」と呼ばれます。**視野を広くして，いろいろな知識を身に着けましょう。**

《 指さし英会話 》

UNIT 1 受付場面の指さし英会話

付録

受付場面でのセリフ

Is this your first visit to this hospital?
この病院に来るのは初めてですか？

Do you have a Japanese medical insurance card?
日本の医療保険証をお持ちですか？

Please fill out this patient form.
こちらの問診票にご記入ください。

受付場面でのコミュニケーション表現

Would you like to ～?
～されたいですか？

I'd like to ～. ～をしたい。

- see a doctor
  医師に診てもらう
- receive a drug
  薬をもらう
- see a medical interpreter
  医療通訳に会う
- have an examination / a medical check-up
  検査・検診をする

• Unit 1 • Is this your first visit to this hospital?

| Do you have (a/an) ～?
～を持っていますか？ | You need to bring (a/an) ～?
～を持ってくる必要があります。 | I have (a/an) ～.
～を持っています。 |

| National Health Insurance
国民健康保険 | private
民間の | insurance
保険 |
| overseas travel insurance
海外旅行保険 | public
公的な | uninsured
保険に未加入の |

| Personal Accident Insurance for Students Pursuing Education and Research
学生教育研究災害傷害保険（学研災） |

イラストでわかる受付場面で必要な書類や証明書

health insurance card　　patient registration card　　patient form　　official identification
健康保険証　　　　　　　　診察券　　　　　　　　　　　問診票　　　　　公的身分証明書

イラストでわかる病院内施設

outpatient reception　　cashier　　pharmacy　　hospital shop
外来受付　　　　　　　　会計　　　　薬局　　　　売店

blood collection room　　X-ray room
採血室　　　　　　　　　　レントゲン室

アメリカ　　　　　　　　　　　　イギリス
the third floor　　3階　　the second floor
the second floor　　2階　　the first floor
the first floor　　1階　　the ground floor

79

UNIT 2 トリアージ場面の指さし英会話

トリアージ場面でのセリフ

What's the matter with you?
どうされましたか？

Do you have a fever?
熱はありますか？

I recommend seeing the ～ department.
～科の受診をお勧めします。

トリアージ場面での体調を伝えるコミュニケーション表現

Do you have (a/an) ～?
～はありますか？

I have (a/an) ～.
～があります。

headache 頭痛	fever 熱	cough 咳	runny nose 鼻水・鼻汁
difficulty in breathing 息が苦しい	shortness of breath 息切れ	hives じんましん	swelling むくみ・浮腫
diarrhea 下痢	itchiness かゆみ・掻痒感	pain 痛み	nausea 吐き気・嘔気
vomiting おう吐	heartburn 胸やけ	bleeding 出血	wheezing 喘鳴

○ ×

• Unit 2 • What's the matter with you?

イラストでわかる診療科一覧

internal medicine
内科

surgery
外科

pediatrics
小児科

orthopedic surgery
整形外科

dermatology
皮膚科

ophthalmology
眼科

otorhinolaryngology
耳鼻咽喉科

obstetrics and gynecology
産婦人科

dentistry
歯科

anesthesiology
麻酔科

radiology
放射線科

urology / dialysis
泌尿器科 / 人工透析

gastroenterology
消化器内科

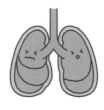
respiratory medicine
呼吸器内科

neurology
神経内科

emergency
救命救急部

81

採血場面の指さし英会話

採血場面でのセリフ

I'm going to take a blood sample.
血液を採らせていただきます。

May I confirm your name and date of birth?
お名前と生年月日を確認させていただけますか？

Have you ever had skin trouble with alcohol wipes?
今までにアルコールティッシュで皮膚が荒れたことはありますか？

Roll up your sleeve. Make a fist with your thumb inside.
袖をまくってください。親指を中に入れて拳を作ってください。

It may sting a little.
すこしチクッとするかもしれません。

We've finished. You can relax now.
終わりましたよ。楽にしてください。

Do not rub the wound.
傷口は揉まないようにしてください。

• Unit 3 • I'm going to take a blood sample

イラストでわかる採血場面で体調を伝える表現

fine
大丈夫

nausea
吐き気

numb
しびれた

painful
痛い

dizzy
めまい

itchy
かゆい

rash
発疹

イラストでわかる採血場面で使う医療器具

glove
手袋

needle
注射針

syringe
注射器

evacuated blood tube
真空採血管

bandage
ばんそうこう

tape
テープ

alcohol wipe
アルコールティッシュ（綿）

tourniquet
駆血帯

sharps container
針捨てボックス

vacuum blood collection tube holder
真空採血管用ホルダー

butterfly needle
翼状針

83

入院オリエンテーション場面の指さし英会話

入院オリエンテーション場面でのセリフ

Let me explain our daily routine.
1日の流れを説明します。

We will come to take your temperature at〜.
〜時に体温を測りに来ます。

The doctor will come soon.
先生（医師）はまもなく来られます。

The doctor will explain the examination.
先生（医師）から検査について説明があります。

入院オリエンテーション場面で使う時間を表すコミュニケーション表現

What time is it?　それは何時ですか？

It's 〜 o'clock.　〜時です。

It's 〜 am.　午前〜時です。

It's 〜 pm.　午後〜時です。

①five fifteen
②fifteen after five
③quarter past five

①five thirty
②この表現は使いません
③half past five

①five forty-five
②fifteen before six
③quarter to six

• Unit 4 • Let me explain our daily routine

イラストでわかる病室にある機器・備品

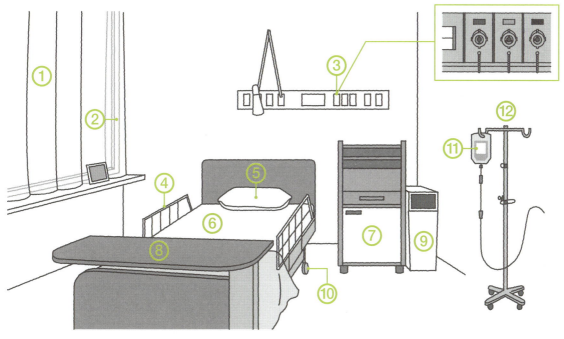

1 **window** 窓   2 **curtain** カーテン   3 **medical gas outlet** 医療ガスアウトレット・中央配管 *
4 **side rail** ベッド柵   5 **pillow** 枕   6 **bed** ベッド   7 **refrigerator** 冷蔵庫
8 **overbed table** オーバーテーブル   9 **garbage bin** ゴミ箱
10 **nurse call button** ナースコール（ボタン）   11 **IV bag** 点滴静注バッグ   12 **IV stand** 点滴スタンド

> **notes**
> 中央配管は色で区別されています。緑は「酸素」，黄色は「空気」，黒が「吸引」です。

イラストでわかる検査

blood test
血液検査

X-ray
レントゲン

computer tomography (CT) scan
CT スキャン

ultrasound scan
超音波スキャン

electrocardiogram
心電図

magnetic resonance imaging
MRI（磁気共鳴画像法）

85

UNIT 5 付録 生活習慣をたずねる場面の指さし英会話

生活習慣をたずねる場面でのコミュニケーション表現

> I'm going to ask you about your lifestyle habits. Do you 〜?
> あなたの生活習慣についてお聞きします。〜されますか？

- **smoke** 喫煙する
- **drink alcohol** 飲酒する
- **exercise** 運動する
- **have allergies** アレルギーがある
- **take medicines** 薬を飲む

> Is/Are there 〜?
> 〜ありますか？

- **religious restrictions** 宗教上の制限
- **anything we should know** 私たちが知っておくべきこと

世界の主な宗教一覧

Buddhism	Christianity	Islam	Judaism	Hinduism
仏教	キリスト教	イスラム教	ユダヤ教	ヒンドゥー教

イラストでわかる宗教関連表現

pork 豚肉

alcohol アルコール

beef 牛肉

pray お祈り

fast 断食

• Unit 5 • I'm going to ask you about your lifestyle habits

生活習慣をたずねる問診票

Do you smoke regularly?
習慣的に，たばこを吸いますか？

□ **No** いいえ   □ **Yes** はい   □ **Used to smoke** 以前吸っていた

Cigarette consumption 喫煙量	Duration of smoking 喫煙期間	Year when you stopped smoking ※ 喫煙をやめた年
_____ cigarettes/Day 本 日	_____ Years 年	_____ Year 年 _____ Month 月

※ If you still have a smoking habit, leave a blank in the question about the year you stopped smoking. 現在も喫煙をされている方は，喫煙をやめた年は空欄のままにしておいてください。

Do you drink regularly?
習慣的にお酒を飲みますか。

□ **No** いいえ   □ **Yes** はい
□ **Used to drink regularly** 以前飲酒する習慣があった。

□ **Beer** ビール   _____ ml/Day 日   □ **Whisky** ウイスキー   _____ ml/Day 日

□ **Japanese sake** 日本酒   _____ ml/Day 日   □ **Wine** ワイン   _____ ml/Day 日

□ **Other(s)** その他   _____ ml/Day 日

If female, answer the questions below.
女性の方のみ以下の質問にお答えください。
Are you pregnant, or possibly pregnant?
妊娠していますか。またその可能性はありますか。

□ **No** いいえ   □ **Yes** はい   □ **Do not know** わからない

Are you breastfeeding?
現在，授乳中ですか。

□ **No** いいえ   □ **Yes** はい

87

UNIT 6 病歴をたずねる場面の指さし英会話 付録

病歴をたずねる場面でのセリフ

Have you had any surgeries before?
以前に手術を受けたことはありますか？

Do you remember when it was?
それがいつか覚えていますか？

How about your parents?
ご両親はどうですか？

Thank you for your cooperation.
ご協力ありがとうございました。

病歴をたずねる場面でのコミュニケーション表現

Have you had ～ before?
以前に～になったことはありますか？

I have had surgery for ～.
～の手術をしたことがあります。

I had ～.
～になりました。

cancer がん	heart attack 心臓発作	fracture 骨折	bleeding 出血	pneumonia 肺炎
ulcer 潰瘍	inflammation 炎症	asthma 喘息	diabetes 糖尿病	osteoporosis 骨粗しょう症
glaucoma 緑内障	cataract 白内障	depression うつ病	impaired hearing 難聴	atopic dermatitis アトピー性皮膚炎

• Unit 6 • Have you had any surgeries before?

イラストでわかる臓器の名称一覧

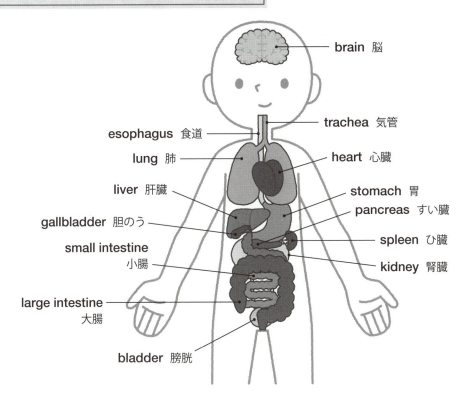

時間を表すコミュニケーション表現

UNIT 7 アレルギーの聞き取り場面の指さし英会話

付録

アレルギーの聞き取り場面でのセリフ

Do you have any allergies?
アレルギーはありますか？

Can you tell me more about that?
それについてより詳しく
教えていただけますか？

We'll make sure to avoid it.
私たちはそれを避けるようにします。

アレルギーの聞き取り場面でのコミュニケーション表現

Do you have 〜?
〜はありますか？

I have 〜.
〜があります。

food allergies 食物アレルギー	drug allergies 薬物アレルギー	alcohol allergies アルコールアレルギー
latex allergies ラテックスアレルギー	insect sting allergies 昆虫刺されアレルギー	dust allergies ほこりアレルギー
mold allergies かびアレルギー	pollen allergies 花粉症	metal allergies 金属アレルギー
seasonal allergies 季節性アレルギー	pet allergies ペットアレルギー	

• Unit 7 • Do you have any allergies?

アレルゲンの聞き取り場面でのコミュニケーション表現

Do you have an allergy to (a/an) 〜?
〜アレルギーはありますか？

I have an allergy to (a/an) 〜.
〜 アレルギーがあります。

egg 卵	milk 牛乳	dairy products 乳製品	wheat 小麦	nuts ナッツ
soy 大豆	shellfish 甲殻類	mold カビ	pollen 花粉	dust mites ダニ
pet dander ペットの毛や皮膚	aspirin アスピリン	latex ラテックス	antibiotics 抗生物質	metal 金属

アレルギー症状の聞き取り場面でのコミュニケーション表現

Did you have 〜?
〜はありましたか？

I had 〜.
〜がありました。

skin rash 発疹	hives じんましん	swelling 腫れ	itching かゆみ
tingling チクチク感	nausea 吐き気	vomiting 嘔吐	cramping 痙攣
dizziness めまい	sneezing くしゃみ	runny nose 鼻水	
loss of consciousness 意識喪失	stuffy nose 鼻づまり	difficulty in breathing 呼吸困難	

91

UNIT 8 痛みについてたずねる場面の指さし英会話

付録

痛みについてたずねる場面でのセリフ

How are you feeling?
体調はいかがですか？

How would you describe your pain?
どのような痛みですか？

How would you rate your pain?
痛みはどれぐらいですか？

When did your pain start?
痛みはいつから始まりましたか？

痛みについてたずねる場面でのコミュニケーション表現

Is it (a/an) ～ pain?
それは～な痛みですか？

I think it is (a/an) ～ pain.
それは～な痛みだと思います。

dull にぶい	sharp するどい	piercing 刺すような	brief darting ずきっと
needle-like チクチク	burning ひりひり	pounding がんがん	throbbing うずく
squeezing しめつけられる	continuous 持続性の	intermittent 断続的な	recurring 反復性の
chronic 慢性の	acute 急性の	tingling ぴりぴり・ちくちく	shooting つきぬけるような	electric shock-like 電気が走るような

• Unit 9 • How much can you move your legs?

可動域の確認場面の指さし英会話

可動域の確認場面でのセリフ

> I'd like to see how much you can move your legs.
> 脚をどれくらい動かせるか見てみたいと思います。

> Could you bring your right thigh toward your chest?
> 右太ももを胸の方に持ってきていただけますか？

> Can you go any further?
> もう少しできますか？

> You're making good progress!
> 順調に進んでいますよ！

イラストでわかる姿勢・動作一覧

lie on one's back
仰向けになる

lie on one's stomach
うつ伏せになる

lie on one's side
横向きになる

sit on the edge of the bed
ベッドの端に座る

bend one's knees
両膝を曲げる

straighten one's knees
両膝を伸ばす

93

体の部位に関する表現

付録

イラストでわかる体の部位

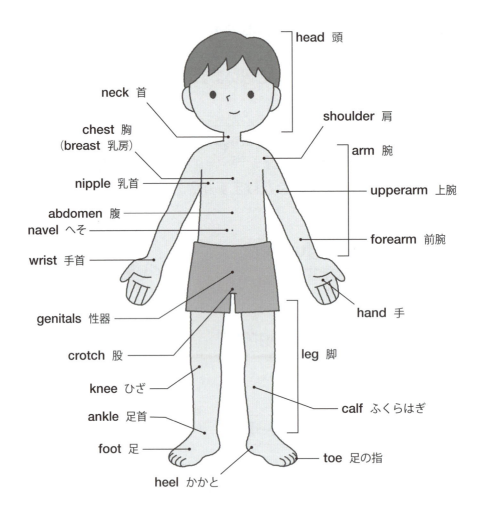

• Unit 10 • Let's start practicing getting into the wheelchair

車椅子への移乗場面の指さし英会話

車椅子への移乗場面でのセリフ

Let's start practicing getting into the wheelchair.
車いすに乗る練習を始めましょう。

Put your arms over my neck.
私の首に腕を回してください。

After I say, "one, two, three", stand up.
1・2・3と言った後に立ってください。

Sit on the wheelchair slowly.
ゆっくり車椅子に座りましょう。

We did a wonderful job!
私たちはよく頑張りました！

95

イラストでわかるリハビリで使う医療器具

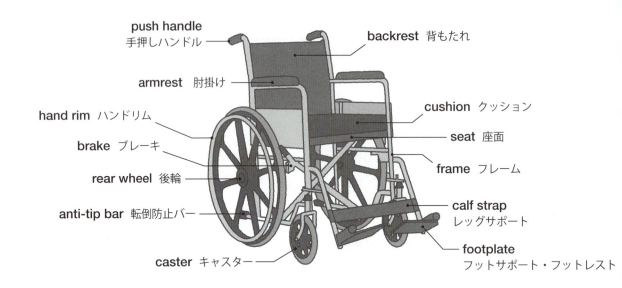

- push handle　手押しハンドル
- backrest　背もたれ
- armrest　肘掛け
- cushion　クッション
- hand rim　ハンドリム
- seat　座面
- brake　ブレーキ
- frame　フレーム
- rear wheel　後輪
- calf strap　レッグサポート
- anti-tip bar　転倒防止バー
- footplate　フットサポート・フットレスト
- caster　キャスター

crutches
松葉杖

Lofstrand crutch
ロフストランド杖

three-legged crutch
3点杖

cane
杖

walker
歩行器

• Unit 11 • Let's make the walks longer

リハビリ場面の指さし英会話

リハビリ場面でのセリフ

I'd like to see how you walk.
どのように歩くか見せてください。

You can use the handrail for support.
手すりを支えに使っても構いません。

You're getting better!
少しずつ良くなっていますよ！

Let's make the walks longer little by little.
少しずつ歩く距離を伸ばしましょう。

イラストでわかるリハビリテーション室にある設備

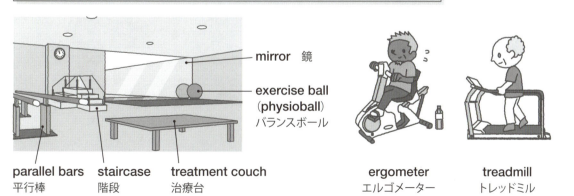

mirror　鏡
exercise ball (physioball)　バランスボール
parallel bars　平行棒
staircase　階段
treatment couch　治療台
ergometer　エルゴメーター
treadmill　トレッドミル

97

■ イラストでわかるリハビリ場面でつかう動作

raise one's arms in the air
腕をあげる

raise (lift) one's shoulders
肩をあげる

roll one's shoulders
肩を回す

turn one's head
頭を左右に向ける

tilt one's head
頭を傾ける

rotate one's head
頭を回す

bend one's arm
腕を曲げる

stretch one's arm
腕を伸ばす

stand on one leg
片足で立つ

• Unit 12-15 • You're from Australia, aren't you?~By working together, we can ease your concerns

UNIT 12-15 感情に関連する英語表現
付録

■ イラストでわかる感情に関連するコミュニケーション表現

What seems to be the problem?
どうされましたか？

I'm ～.
私は～です。

| happy 幸せな | confident 自信がある | surprised おどろいた | sad 悲しい | nervous 緊張した | angry 怒った | bored 退屈した |

| peaceful 穏やかな | excited 興奮した | relaxed リラックスした | lonely 寂しい | embarrassed 恥ずかしい | worried 心配した | frustrated イライラした |

| joyful 楽しい | glad うれしい | comfortable 快適な | shocked ショックを受けた | mad 怒った | disappointed 失望した | ashamed 恥ずかしい |

■ 感情に関連する程度を表す表現

| a little 少し | very とても |

| always いつも | often よく | usually 普段 | sometimes 時々 |

| never 決して～ない | rarely めったに～ない | not often あまり～ない |

99

あいづちに関連する英語表現

あいづちに関連するコミュニケーション表現

| I see.
なるほど。 | Exactly.
その通りです。 | Really?
そうなんですか？ |

That's right.
そうですね。

That's true.
確かにそうですね。

Me too.
私もそうですよ。

Is that so?
そうなのですか。

I think so too.
私もそう思います。

That must be 〜.
それは〜に違いないですね。

You must be 〜.
あなたは〜に違いないですね。

TEXT PRODUCTION STAFF

edited by	編集
Mitsugu Shishido	宍戸　貢

English-language editing by	英文校閲
Bill Benfield	ビル・ベンフィールド

text & cover design by	本文および表紙デザイン
Nobuyoshi Fujino	藤野　伸芳

typesetting & illustrated by	組版およびイラスト作成
Marin Crane	有限会社マーリンクレイン

Medical Advisors	医療アドバイザー
Takeshi Hata	畑剛史
Yoshinari Okamoto	岡本佳也

CD PRODUCTION STAFF

narrated by	吹き込み者
Karen Haedrich（AmE）	カレン・ヘドリック（アメリカ英語）
Howard Colefield（AmE）	ハワード・コルフィールド（アメリカ英語）

Care for All
― Effective Patient Communication for Healthcare Workers ―
医療従事者のためのやさしい英語コミュニケーション

2025 年 1 月 20 日　初版発行
2025 年 2 月 15 日　第 2 刷発行

著　者　田中　博晃
　　　　眞砂　薫

発行者　佐野　英一郎

発行所　株式会社　成美堂
　　　　〒101-0052　東京都千代田区神田小川町 3-22
　　　　TEL 03-3291-2261　FAX 03-3293-5490
　　　　https://www.seibido.co.jp

印刷・製本　株式会社　加藤文明社

ISBN 978-4-7919-7319-4　　　　　　　　　　　　Printed in Japan

・落丁・乱丁本はお取り替えします。
・本書の無断複写は，著作権上の例外を除き著作権侵害となります。